I0819537

PRAISE FOR

DIAMOND FEVER!

"Steve Sheinkin is more than an author—he's a time traveler whose deep research and fabulous writing whisk readers on thrilling rides through history. Kids will be transfixed by this unbelievable-but-true story of Gilded Age diamond hunters, swindlers, and train robbers. It is one of my absolute favorites!"

—Lauren Tarshis, bestselling author of the *I Survived* series

ALSO BY STEVE SHEINKIN

"Master of fast-paced histories." —*The Washington Post*

IMPOSSIBLE ESCAPE
A True Story of Survival and Heroism in Nazi Germany

FALLOUT
Spies, Superbombs, and the Ultimate Cold War Showdown

BORN TO FLY
The First Women's Air Race Across America

UNDEFEATED
Jim Thorpe and the Carlisle Indian School Football Team

MOST DANGEROUS
Daniel Ellsberg and the Secret History of the Vietnam War

BOMB
The Race to Build—and Steal—the World's Most Dangerous Weapon

THE PORT CHICAGO 50
Disaster, Mutiny, and the Fight for Civil Rights

THE NOTORIOUS BENEDICT ARNOLD
A True Story of Adventure, Heroism & Treachery

WHICH WAY TO THE WILD WEST?
Everything Your Schoolbooks Didn't Tell You About America's Westward Expansion

TWO MISERABLE PRESIDENTS
Everything Your Schoolbooks Didn't Tell You About the Civil War

KING GEORGE: WHAT WAS HIS PROBLEM?
Everything Your Schoolbooks Didn't Tell You About the American Revolution

DIAMOND FEVER!

DIAMOND FEVER!

A TRUE CRIME STORY IN THE WILD WEST

STEVE SHEINKIN

with comics and art by Jon Chad

ROARING BROOK PRESS
NEW YORK

Published by Roaring Brook Press
Roaring Brook Press is a division of Holtzbrinck Publishing Holdings Limited Partnership
120 Broadway, New York, NY 10271 • mackids.com

EU representative: Macmillan Publishers Ireland Ltd, 1st Floor, The Liffey Trust Centre, 117–126 Sheriff Street Upper, Dublin 1, D01 YC43

Our books may be purchased in bulk for specialty retail/wholesale, literacy, corporate/premium, educational, and subscription box use. Please contact MacmillanSpecialMarkets@macmillan.com.

Library of Congress Control Number 2025028943

First edition, 2026
Book design by Aurora Parlagreco
Printed in the United States of America by Lakeside Book Company, Harrisonburg, Virginia

ISBN 978-1-250-26574-6
10 9 8 7 6 5 4 3 2

FOR DAVID,

travel partner on the road to Diamond Peak

CONTENTS

Cast of Characters x

Prologue: The Wild West 1

Part 1: ROUGH DIAMONDS 4

1. The Secret 11
2. Lucky Find 14
3. The Partners 18
4. The Pirates 25
5. City in a Hurry 32
6. The Wild West, Part 2 38

Part 2: BIG MONEY 40

7. The Cousins Return 45
8. Dazzling Light 51
9. The Gilded Age 58
10. Long Winter 63

Part 3: BEYOND CALCULATION 68

11. Happy Mood 75
12. Wild Scramble 82
13. Diamonds and Salt 85
14. The Wild East 92
15. California Street 95
16. The Country Gentleman 100

Part 4: GEOLOGIST IN CHARGE 102
17. Clarence King 109
18. Competing Claims 113
19. Two Arnolds 119
20. Two Expeditions 125

Part 5: BRILLIANT CITY 132
21. Glitter and Flash 139
22. The Diamondiferous Locality 145
23. Carboniferous Fossils 149
24. Full Believers 154

Part 6: KING OF DIAMONDS 158
25. Startling Facts 163
26. The Wild East, Part 2 169
27. Befooled 171
28. Salted! 177
29. The Chief Salter 180
30. The Fever Breaks 186

Epilogue: Pretty Stones 192
Author's Note 205
Source Notes 211
Bibliography 225
Index 235

CAST OF CHARACTERS

PHILIP ARNOLD

JOHN SLACK

GEORGE ROBERTS

ASBURY HARPENDING

CLARENCE KING

HENRY JANIN

MARY ARNOLD

ALFRED RUBERY

A. D. WILSON

CHARLES TIFFANY

JAMES MARRYATT

SAMUEL EMMONS

WILLIAM LENT

WILLIAM RALSTON

J. F. BERRY

BEN BUTLER

GEORGE S. DODGE

MIKE GRAY

SUSAN B. ANTHONY

HORACE GREELEY

PROLOGUE

THE WILD WEST

Even train robbers have to wait for their train.

About an hour after midnight on November 5, 1870, five men with bandanas tied over their faces huddled by the tracks in Verdi, Nevada. It was a freezing night, with a dusting of snow on the hard ground. Finally, the men saw what they were waiting for—the beam of a train's headlamp, growing brighter as it approached. The eastbound train, loaded with payroll for miners in nearby Virginia City, stopped briefly in Verdi.

As it clattered out of town, the masked men leapt aboard.

Led by A. J. Davis, the gang detached the passenger cars at the back of the train. These cars, and their snoozing travelers, fell behind and were soon out of sight. Pulling pistols from their belts, the bandits forced the engineer to drive on. Davis stopped what was left of the train at a remote spot between Verdi and Reno. His men banged on the door of the express car, where valuable shipments were stored.

"Who's there?" asked the guard inside.

One of the gang growled "Marshall"—the name of the train's conductor.

The lock clicked open. The thieves charged in, disarming the guard and busting open strongboxes. They tossed sacks of $20 gold coins into the brush by the side of the rails, jumped down, divvied up the plunder, and rode off on horses they'd stashed nearby—leaving tracks in the shallow snow.

The entire gang was chased down and captured. Lawmen forced A. J. Davis to lead them to the spot where he'd hidden his loot, a clump of sagebrush near a bridge over the Truckee River. An officer kicked away loose dirt, uncovering a freshly dug hole. Davis looked on, "sick at heart," as one newspaper writer put it, at the sight of gold coins glinting in the sun.

All of the stolen money was recovered—except for 150 coins, which one of the thieves claimed to have buried somewhere on the banks of the Truckee. People have been searching for this treasure ever since. The gold alone in each coin is worth over $3,000 today, and the actual coins, with their unique history, would be worth *far* more than that.

As far as we know, they're still out there.

Meanwhile, the Verdi heist went down in history as the first train robbery west of the Rocky Mountains. The gang had stolen $41,600, over a million dollars in today's money. This was exactly the sort of crime—masked bandits, bags of gold, horses and lawmen and buried treasure—that would be dramatized in magazines and stage plays in the late 1800s, in movies and comics in the 1900s. It was a crime that helped create the image of the Wild West.

But it was nothing compared to the crime about to begin in San Francisco.

PART 1

ROUGH DIAMONDS

San Francisco, California

November 1870

George Roberts, an investor in gold and silver mines, was working late.

Roberts knew these two men. He'd worked with them before.
CREEEAK

Philip Arnold
John Slack

They'd been out prospecting, Arnold explained. They'd found... something.

Something they could not risk carrying around. Might they lock it in Roberts's safe overnight?

What's in it?

CLUNK

CLUNK

Diamonds.

1

THE SECRET

Diamonds?

Yeah, maybe.

"Rough diamonds," Philip Arnold added, gesturing to the stones he had just poured onto George Roberts's desk. Uncut diamonds, in other words. Unpolished. Not ready to be sold as jewelry—but still, very valuable gems.

Was that possible? To Roberts, these "rough diamonds" looked like glassy gray pebbles. Nothing near the glittering jewels rich folks wore to the opera house. Was this how diamonds looked when they came out of the ground?

George Roberts had no idea.

He knew the men standing in his office, though: Philip Arnold and John Slack. Cousins from Kentucky who'd been kicking around the West for years, hunting for gold and silver—and sometimes finding it. Small-timers, but tough guys. Good miners.

Roberts asked his visitors where they'd found the stones.

Arnold, normally bursting with jokes and tales of adventure, was annoyingly quiet. He'd only say that he and Slack had been looking for gold out in, well . . . somewhere in the West. The important thing was, they'd unearthed these gems and weren't comfortable carrying them around San Francisco. The banks were closed. They needed a safe, and Roberts had one.

A believable story. But *diamonds*? Had these cousins really discovered a diamond mine?

No one had found diamonds in the American West, though folks figured they must be out there. "It may not pay to hunt for diamonds," a California geologist advised miners, "yet it always pays to pick them up when you do happen to see them."

Right. Very helpful.

Anyway, Roberts was interested. He agreed to lock the bag in his safe.

Philip Arnold had one more request. A demand, in fact: total silence from George Roberts. Until the cousins figured out what to do with the jewels, their existence must be kept secret. Roberts agreed.

The cousins left their bag in George Roberts's safe.

Their secret didn't last twelve hours.

2

LUCKY FIND

Some secrets just never have a chance.

Twenty-two years earlier, at a small settlement soon to become the city of Sacramento, California, a wealthy landowner named John Sutter was working at his desk when a visitor charged in. Sutter looked up and saw a carpenter he'd hired, James Marshall, dripping and dirty from galloping through the rain. Marshall was supposed to be building a sawmill on the nearby American River. Sutter wondered why the man had left his work.

"Are you alone?" Marshall asked.

"Yes," Sutter said.

"Did you lock the door?"

"No, but I will if you wish it."

Once the door was secured, Marshall pulled out a sack, poured the contents into the palm of his hand, and said, "I believe this is gold."

Sutter examined the yellow grains and flakes. Quite heavy for their size. He got an encyclopedia off the shelf, read the entry on gold, and performed a few of the recommended experiments. One easy test is to bite the metal—pure gold is so soft, you can leave a tooth mark.

This was the real thing.

Sutter hoped to keep a lid on the secret, but carpenters at the worksite knew of Marshall's discovery. They were a lot more excited about finding gold than building some rich guy's sawmill. Word spread fast, setting off the California Gold Rush, with hundreds of thousands of people racing in from all over the world. Gold was found in fabulous amounts, sparking a major economic boom and fueling the rise of the city at the heart of it all, San Francisco. This was a disaster for Native Americans, who saw settlers swarm onto their land and establish a government that had no respect for their rights or freedom. Like all major events in American history, the Gold Rush was huge, complex, and messy.

And it all started with someone showing up in an office and pulling something interesting from his pocket . . .

Had the same thing just happened to George Roberts? The question was impossible to avoid.

Roberts knew about the Gold Rush—he'd lived it. Raised

in Ohio, terrified of being trapped in boring offices forever, Roberts fled west in his early twenties. He waded through frigid rivers and scrambled up rugged hills searching for the glint of gold. And he actually found it. Roberts filed a claim on a promising piece of land but lacked the cash to work the mine. He wound up selling it to a large company for $350—worth about $15,000 today. A tidy profit, or so it seemed at the time.

The mine would prove to be one of the richest in California, producing nearly six million ounces of gold. The lesson Roberts learned was this: Any fool can trip on a lucky find. The one with the money and the vision to seize control—that's who gets rich in this game.

Now in his early forties, George Roberts badly wanted to be that guy. He *needed* to be. A short man with a graying goatee and gentle eyes, he had several projects going, mining investments that weren't paying off. He was drowning in debt, facing payments he couldn't make. "I am at the end of my tether," he confided to a friend. "I am continually at a strain to keep up appearances."

In another note he sounded even more distressed, confessing, "I am busted sure."

What Roberts needed was a bit of luck. So . . . *had* these cousins from Kentucky tripped on a lucky find? Could the stones in their bag be genuine diamonds?

You couldn't bite a diamond, Roberts knew. Well, you

could, but it was a lousy idea. Diamonds are extremely hard—hard enough to cut glass. But couldn't other minerals do that too? The pebbles in Roberts's safe were likely worthless quartz crystals. An understandable mistake by long-suffering miners who thought they'd finally struck it rich.

But what if Arnold and Slack were right?

What if they'd stumbled into a second Sutter's Mill? Or something bigger, if that could be imagined? Diamonds, after all, were even more valuable per ounce than gold.

The temptation was too great. The morning after Arnold and Slack's visit, George Roberts did the one thing he'd promised not to do. Opening his safe, he grabbed the bag of stones and stepped out into the busy city.

Horse-drawn carriages bounced down wide cobblestone streets. Roberts hurried past office buildings and hotels, saloons and billiard halls. Bank windows displayed colorful currencies from around the world. In the windows of mining offices were samples of gold and silver ore, with labels naming the mines and inviting investors to get in on once-in-a-lifetime opportunities. Competing newsboys waved papers and shouted the day's headlines.

George Roberts didn't want to know the news. He wanted to see a jeweler.

3

THE PARTNERS

Roberts heard back from his jeweler friend. The stones he'd dropped off were genuine diamonds.

He took them to another respected jeweler. Same result.

The diamonds were "in the rough," as Arnold had said. The stones would need to be skillfully cut and polished to sparkle like gems on a pricey necklace. That sort of work was done in a few European cities such as London, Amsterdam, and Antwerp. There was not a single diamond expert west of the Mississippi River.

This was all very interesting to Roberts, and it sparked lots of new questions.

1. Where exactly had these diamonds been found?
2. How many more might be out there?
3. Could Roberts get control of the mine before the secret got out?

Roberts had worked with the Kentucky cousins before. The fancy-suit types in San Francisco saw Slack and Arnold as country bumpkins, but Roberts knew they were skillful prospectors. In fact, Roberts owed Arnold $20,000 for a share of a silver mine the cousins had found in New Mexico—yet another of the debts ruining his life. Well, the silver mine could wait. For now, Roberts needed to know more about the diamonds Arnold and Slack had found.

He called the cousins back to his office for an urgent meeting.

Philip Arnold was forty years old in 1870, with blue-gray eyes and a playful, boyish face beneath his scruffy mustache. Born on a farm near Elizabethtown, Kentucky, Phil was only five when his mother died. His father struggled with alcoholism and couldn't support the family. At sixteen, Phil was apprenticed to a hatmaker, a cruel man better known for his foul language than for the quality of his headwear. Phil ran off to New Orleans, enlisted in the army, and served in the Mexican-American War. He then joined the rush to California before returning home to marry a childhood friend named Mary May. Phil and Mary now lived in San Francisco with three children, ages eleven, nine, and six.

John Slack was a bachelor, nine years older than Arnold. Tall and lean, with a short beard, he was also a Mexican-American

War vet—and a distant relation to Abraham Lincoln's family back in Kentucky. Slack had spent most of the past twenty years in the Southwest, even serving a term in the Arizona Territorial House of Representatives. Personality-wise, the cousins were opposites. Arnold was a fast-talker, a dealmaker; Slack was quiet, steady, dependable.

When the cousins returned to his office, George Roberts failed to mention that he'd taken the stones out of his safe and had them tested. But this must have been obvious to Slack and Arnold. Otherwise why was Roberts so excited? So anxious to know more about their find?

Much to Roberts's irritation, the cousins clammed up again. Where had they found their bag of stones? Somewhere in "Indian territory"—that's all they'd say.

That could be anywhere. Wasn't it all Indian territory?

At the end of the United States' war with Mexico in 1848, American leaders forced Mexico to sign a treaty turning over much of what became the vast American West: the present-day states of California, Nevada, and Utah, and parts of Texas, New Mexico, Arizona, Colorado, Wyoming, Oklahoma, and Kansas. An estimated three hundred thousand Native Americans already lived on this land. The West was home to hundreds of Indian nations, as it had been long before Europeans arrived.

So "Indian territory" didn't narrow it down much. Could the cousins be a bit more specific?

They could not, Arnold informed Roberts.

They'd found the mine, and they meant to hold on to it. They'd keep its location secret until they figured out what to do next. In any case, winter weather was setting in, and no serious mining could be done until spring.

Meanwhile, since the stones had obviously been tested, rumors of a diamond strike were likely to leak. Roberts suggested a strategy—they'd spread the word that upon further inspection, the hoped-for gems had proved to be worthless.

The cousins agreed. They took back their bag of diamonds and left.

Roberts was near panic. Was the chance of a lifetime slipping through his hands? Frantic for help and advice, he fired off a telegram to his business partner, Asbury Harpending.

Asbury Harpending—not only a great name but the name that would come to be most closely associated with this legendary crime story. Harpending would spend the rest of his life trying to explain his role in the stunning events about to unfold.

For now, he was on his way to London on business. Roberts's first telegram reached him in New York City. "Arnold has returned," Roberts reported. "He made a great discovery of diamonds. Are keeping it quiet."

Blank No. 7.

THE WESTERN UNION TELEGRAPH COMPANY

THOS. T KOKERT. Gen'l Sup't. New York

WILLIAM ORTON Pre't. O.H. PALMER. Sec'y. New York

Dated Dec. 1 1870:

Received at New York City

To A. Harpending

Arnold has returned. He made a great discovery of diamonds. Are keeping it quiet.

Harpending would later say that he didn't take the news too seriously. Roberts was a desperate man, probably grasping at straws. Harpending sailed to London as planned. He rented an office and went to work trying to interest English investors in shares of American gold and silver mines.

The urgent notes from Roberts kept coming. This was surprising, in part because of the high cost of sending messages via the new telegraph line running under the Atlantic Ocean between Europe and North America.

The content of the notes was also pretty unusual.

"I have great hopes from this discovery and believe we can

make millions," Roberts cabled. "In the meantime, what is to happen, I can't say."

Roberts wanted Harpending back in San Francisco, the sooner the better. The clock was ticking. When winter ended, thousands of miners would fan out across the West, as they did every year. Any greenhorn could get lucky and trip onto Slack and Arnold's find.

Harpending had spent years as a miner himself. He knew the thrill of the hunt. "Could it really be true," he'd recall wondering that winter, "that there was a place where diamonds could be picked up on ant hills?" It was like a scene from a fairy tale!

At thirty-one, with a bushy black beard that made him look a bit older, Harpending was a seasoned risk-taker, a juggler of gambles. Like Roberts, he lived on the brink of disaster—but unlike his partner, he relished it. He'd made and lost fortunes and always seemed confident that something would turn up.

Maybe it just had, in the shape of diamonds.

Without mentioning specifics, Harpending confided in an English friend, Alfred Rubery. Harpending told Rubery that his partner in San Francisco seemed to think they were on to a major find—in Harpending's words, "something that would astonish the world."

"Silver?" guessed Rubery.

No, Harpending said. A whole lot bigger than silver.

Rubery urged his friend to sail for America. "Personally, I am bored to death, just pining for a little bit of excitement," he told Harpending. "I will go along with you, and we will stir up things again in the Far West."

Note that Rubery says they'd stir things up *again*.

These two had a history of making trouble in California.

4
THE PIRATES

Born in Kentucky in 1839, Asbury Harpending was a bright student, tall and strikingly handsome, with piercing eyes and thick black hair. At age fifteen, already enrolled in college but too restless to sit in class, Asbury heard about a group of "young gentlemen," as he generously called them, who planned to travel to Central America and conquer the country of Nicaragua. He bolted from school to join this despicable plot and was arrested as he sailed down the Mississippi River.

Harpending would later laugh off this episode as a typical boyish adventure.

He managed to escape and make his way back to Kentucky, where clashes with his father became more and more frequent. With just five dollars in his pocket he lit out again, chasing the lure of riches to California. At sixteen, Harpending dove into the world of mining and speculation, buying and selling shares of gold and silver mines in California, Nevada, and Mexico. He was brash, tireless, risk loving, and lucky. By age seventeen, he had $60,000 in the bank.

At twenty, he had $250,000—nearly $10 million in today's money.

Settling in San Francisco in 1860, Harpending eagerly followed news of that year's bitterly contested presidential election. Abraham Lincoln won—but Southern leaders rejected Lincoln's victory, largely because Lincoln opposed allowing slavery in the territories of the West. Eleven Southern states seceded from the Union, splitting the United States apart and igniting the Civil War.

Harpending declared his support for the rebels of the South. Was he actually pro-slavery? Was he just defying his dad, a strong Union man? A bit of both? That's not totally clear, but we do know he poured cash into secret groups plotting to break California away from the Union. It was in this shadowy underworld that he first met Alfred Rubery.

Rubery was in his late teens, the son of rich parents in England. He'd run off in search of adventure in the West. He too supported the Confederates in the Civil War, and was, apparently, quite obnoxious about it. One night, while shooting his mouth off in a San Francisco saloon, Rubery said something that infuriated a U.S. Army officer named Lieutenant Tompkins. "High words followed," Harpending would later write, "and Tompkins made a remark that touched Rubery's honor."

Rubery proclaimed, "You will hear from me, sir."

Which meant: *You and I shall now duel to the death.*

Rubery asked Harpending to be his "second"—meaning it was Harpending's job to help prepare his friend for the showdown. Harpending asked Rubery how skilled he was with a sword. "He admitted that he had some knowledge of carving ham," Harpending recalled. So they tried a little pistol practice. "With extra good luck," reported Harpending, "at ten paces he could hit a barn."

This did not bode well for Rubery's chances of survival.

Harpending had coffee with the lieutenant's second and managed to patch things up, getting the duel called off just in time. He and Rubery were now fast friends. They still wanted to help the South win the Civil War.

So they decided to become pirates.

It was common knowledge that millions of dollars in gold were regularly shipped from California to the U.S. government in the East. The country's economy, especially in wartime, was reliant on that gold. So why not steal it?

This was Harpending's plan. After all, the American military had only a tiny force in California: a few hundred soldiers in San Francisco and on Alcatraz Island just offshore.

"Now we're getting somewhere," Rubery said. "Count me in to the limit."

The friends bought a schooner, the *Chapman*. They recruited a crew and loaded the *Chapman* with cannons, guns, and swords. The plan was to sail to an island off the coast of Mexico and lie in wait. Ships laden with California gold would pass that way en route to the East Coast—and they'd grab one. Everything was set.

Just one slight snag: No one aboard knew anything about

the geography of coastal Mexico. Harpending hired an experienced navigator named William Law.

Now they were set. If only they could get out of San Francisco without arousing suspicion.

On the dark, overcast night of March 14, 1863, Harpending and Rubery met in an alley behind a downtown hotel. Darting past roaring saloons and gambling halls, they got down to the waterfront and aboard the *Chapman*. The crew was ready. The wind and tide conditions were right. They could cruise out of the bay before sunrise. As soon as the navigator showed up, that is. He was late. They really couldn't leave without him. None of the crew had ever steered anything larger than a rowboat.

The ship rocked gently in the harbor. Midnight came and went. Two a.m. No sign of William Law.

The pirates fell asleep.

When daylight woke them, Harpending saw boatloads of American soldiers approaching, along with a tugboat full of San Francisco police. He shook Rubery awake. The two friends lit a fire on the cabin floor, attempting to burn incriminating documents, shoving some of the papers in their mouths as the law closed in.

Harpending and Rubery were tossed into separate cells on Alcatraz Island.

The next morning, Harpending heard tapping on the plaster wall of his tiny cell. A voice called: "That you, Harpending?"

He recognized the voice. His long-lost navigator, William Law.

"I'm under arrest," Law said through the wall. "I want to tell you all about the awful mishap that prevented me from being with you on the *Chapman* last night."

Harpending, a self-professed hothead, boiled with rage. He guessed (correctly, as it turned out) that Law had snitched on him to the government and had come to gather more incriminating evidence. What Law didn't know was that Harpending had a knife and small pistol hidden inside his clothes.

Harpending poked his blade through the wall's soft plaster. He lifted the barrel of his loaded gun.

"Law," he said, "there is something I want you to hear very distinctly, and I don't want to speak loud. Put your ear to this hole I have made."

Harpending waited with his finger on the trigger, hoping to hear Law's face touch the wall.

Law must have sensed danger. There was no sound for several minutes.

Finally, Harpending heard Law leaving the cell.

Harpending and Rubery were convicted of treason and sentenced to ten years in prison—but served only a few months. In late 1863, President Lincoln issued a general amnesty to rebels who swore an oath of allegiance to the Union. Harpending made the promise and got out of jail. Rubery was not a U.S. citizen and so ineligible for amnesty. Luckily for him, his wealthy family appealed directly to the White House for a favor. Rubery was put on a ship and sent home to England.

Harpending's fortune was gone, confiscated by the government. He quickly made another, building a fine home and several commercial buildings in San Francisco, strolling the city in elegant clothes, swinging a decorative walking stick. He married a woman named Ira Anna Thompson, and they started a family.

It wasn't enough. He had much bigger dreams.

Now, in the spring of 1871, his pal Rubery at his side, Asbury Harpending sailed back into one of the most spectacular natural harbors on earth, San Francisco Bay.

Time to stir things up in the West once again.

5

CITY IN A HURRY

Harpending stepped off his ship and into the clamor and chaos of the city he called home. Porters raced up demanding to carry passengers' bags in exchange for tips. Cabmen roared offers of rides to any spot in the city. Roving peddlers hawked baskets of fruit, fish, flowers, razors, cough remedies—even loans.

Frisco, as residents affectionately called it, was the first big American city on the West Coast, a fast-growing mix of fancy town and Wild West. You'd see ladies and gentlemen in the latest Paris fashions next to miners spitting tobacco juice. Bankers shoved their way down crowded streets, stepping on toes with no apology. Crews were putting up new buildings everywhere, working their way up the town's steep hills, sending clouds of dust into the city's steady winds. No one stayed clean for long.

Tourists clogged the sidewalks, reading from travel guides and taking in sweeping views of San Francisco Bay: the islands and ships, pelicans diving for fish, sea lions barking on the rocks. Visitors were told to look out for the famous Ben Butler, a fifteen-foot sea lion named for a whiskered member of Congress from Massachusetts whom he supposedly resembled.

Of the city's population of 150,000, only half were born in the United States. "In walking two blocks," wrote one journalist, "you may hear every leading language of Europe, Asia, and America." Just a few years before, thousands of young immigrants from China had done most of the work of building railroads across California and Nevada, blasting tunnels through rugged mountains and laying track across the burning desert. Many had settled in San Francisco, establishing North America's first Chinatown, a bustling neighborhood of shops and restaurants, theaters and small factories.

Asbury Harpending may have been raised in Kentucky, but Frisco—a city built on gold and risky dreams—Frisco was his town. He fed on the city's restless energy, the contagious feeling that anything was possible. That the next big thing was always right around the corner.

Like diamonds, for example.

Harpending went to see his old pal George Roberts. The partners discussed the diamond discovery and agreed on the need for fast action.

But Philip Arnold told Harpending the same thing he'd been telling Roberts all winter—no thanks. "I then refused to sell my interest," Arnold later explained, "or any part of it at any price."

John Slack seemed at least open to negotiation. For now, though, he followed his cousin's lead.

Harpending was not willing to wait—couldn't afford to wait. Snow was melting in the western mountains. How long until some other lucky bumpkin stumbled onto the diamonds? He and Roberts had to get control of the mine while its location was still secret.

In need of added firepower—and serious cash—Harpending brought in William Ralston, founder of the Bank of California. Ralston called the cousins into his grand office, with its arched windows and huge paintings of California redwoods. In this intimidating setting, the banker explained to the boys from Kentucky how things worked. Finding a promising mine was well and good, Ralston lectured. But to do the job right, one needed to legally claim the land, buy tools and equipment, hire engineers and workers and guards. All of this was terribly expensive, far beyond the means of the cousins. Ralston might, just *might*, be willing to invest. "Before we close the deal," the banker said, "we will have to inspect the mines."

At this suggestion, Slack and Arnold went silent. Meeting over.

Finally, under relentless pressure from Harpending and his wealthy friends, Slack agreed to sell half of his share of the diamond mine for $50,000. This was a fortune, well over $1 million in today's money. As to the mine's location—that information wasn't part of the bargain. Arnold and Slack did agree, however, to travel to their secret spot and bring back a large sample of precious stones. This would be all the proof anyone could need of the richness of their find.

Everyone liked the deal. Except Mary Arnold.

Mary had agreed to move to California with her husband, but she worried about the hazards Phil faced while prospecting in remote mountains and deserts. "His life was continually in danger from the life he led," she would later testify, "and was liable to be lost at any moment."

Mary was known as a quiet, intelligent woman. A few years

before, she'd asked for more control over the family's finances. Phil signed a letter giving his wife full legal power, an unusual agreement for the time.

Now, early in the summer of 1871, Mary was heard fighting with her husband, pleading with him not to set off on yet another far-flung mining quest. She even took the step of going to George Roberts's office. She knew Roberts owed her husband $20,000 from a previous deal and begged him not to turn over the money.

Or, in any case, not to give it to Phil to fund his latest goose chase. As Mary insisted, if the money was to be paid, it should legally go to her. Roberts tried to make peace between the warring couple, with no success. Finally, Mary and Phil agreed to separate. Mary got the $20,000. With the cash in hand, she and the children left San Francisco.

Phil Arnold went ahead with his plan to visit the mine. Using some of John Slack's money, the cousins bought supplies and packed their bags. They rode a ferry across the bay to Oakland, watching to make sure they were not followed. Then they got on a train and started east.

6

THE WILD WEST, PART 2

That same month, June 1871, a twenty-four-year-old bandit named Jesse James rode with his gang into the town of Corydon, Iowa. The streets were oddly deserted. A political meeting was being held at a local church, and most folks were over there—including nearly all the employees of the Ocobock Brothers' Bank.

James led his men into the bank. A single cashier stood behind the counter. The crooks pointed pistols at the man, forcing him to hand over keys to the safe. The James gang stuffed about $6,000 into a sack, tied and gagged the cashier, and made their escape.

On their way out of town, James couldn't resist taunting the law-abiding citizens of Iowa. Interrupting the speaker at the public meeting, he announced that someone, for some reason, had tied up the bank's cashier.

"If y'all ain't too busy," James reportedly said, "you might ride over and untie him. I've got to be going."

The speaker, ignoring this rude interruption, went right on lecturing about the vital importance of railroads to the local economy. Half an hour later, when people returned to the bank, they found the cashier hog-tied on the floor. A posse galloped after the thieves but never caught them.

Jesse James was on his way to becoming one of America's most notorious outlaws. Like the Verdi train robbery, this was exactly the sort of big, bold crime we think of when we imagine America's Wild West.

But it was nothing compared to the crime already underway in San Francisco.

PART 2

BIG MONEY

Over one billion years ago . . .

In Earth's upper mantle, under enormous heat and pressure, some carbon atoms locked into very tight crystal structures—diamonds. The incredible natural conditions for their formation are in part what leads to their tremendous value.

CRUST
Ranges from 3 to 25 miles thick

MANTLE
1,800 miles thick on average

OUTER CORE
1,400 miles thick on average

INNER CORE
800 miles thick

Even a small diamond is made up of billions of carbon atoms.

Pencil graphite is also comprised of carbon atoms, but they are formed into a different structure.

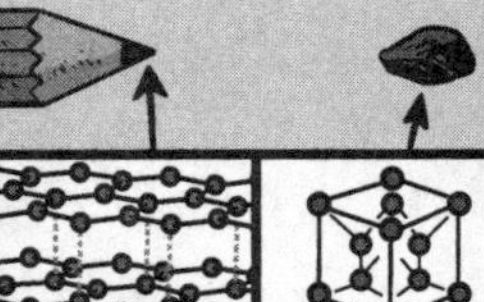

Diamonds are the hardest naturally occurring mineral on Earth, a perfect 10 on the Mohs hardness scale.

Volcanic eruptions rooted deep beneath the surface blasted liquid rock upward—sometimes carrying diamonds.
CRUST
MANTLE
The magma cooled, hardening into rock formations known as kimberlite pipes. Most pipes do not contain diamonds—but some do.
CRUST

Throughout most of human history, nearly all the world's diamonds were found in India.
In the 1700s, miners searching for gold in Brazil were shocked to find what turned out to be diamonds.
SPLISH
SWISH
In the late 1860s, a third major source of diamonds was found—South Africa.
The South African diamond discoveries inspired dreams of quick riches in America.
GIRL IN AFRICA FINDS DIAMOND THE SIZE OF A GOOSE EGG!

In towns across the West, miners began showing up with stones they hoped were diamonds and rubies.

Not a diamond—it's a common quartz crystal.
The "rubies" turned out to be garnets.
But the question remained: Were there untold riches still waiting to be discovered?
Were there diamonds and other precious gems in the vast American West?
CHUGGA CHUGGA
And if so, where were they?

7

THE COUSINS RETURN

Were there diamonds in the West? And if so, where? Philip Arnold had been obsessed with these questions for years.

In the late 1860s, before he and Slack brought their bag of stones to George Roberts's office, Arnold worked as an assistant bookkeeper for A. J. Severance & Co. in San Francisco. The firm used real diamonds, the hardest substance in nature, to manufacture tools such as drill bits and glass cutters. Arnold's job was to help with the account ledgers.

He found diamonds a lot more interesting.

In his free time, Arnold peppered his boss, J. B. Cooper, with questions. "He seemed to take a great interest," Cooper would recall, "in ascertaining the proper tests to distinguish the precious gems."

Cooper suggested articles and books to read. Arnold learned about the German mineralogist Friedrich Mohs, who developed the Mohs scale in 1812. Still in use today, the Mohs scale ranks the hardness of minerals from 1 to 10, with 10 being the hardest. Talc, for instance, is 1 on the scale. Rubies are 9, and diamonds are 10. For comparison, a human fingernail is 2.5. A glass window is 5.5; a steel nail, 6.5.

The important thing, as far as Arnold could tell, was that a harder mineral will always scratch a softer one. This meant miners in search of diamonds could perform a very simple test. "The first thing to be looked after when a suspected stone is found, is to see whether it will cut glass or quartz with its sharp edge," recommended the magazine *Mining and Scientific Press*. "A diamond will do so readily."

Another test would be to subject a suspected diamond to extreme heat. Like other forms of carbon—coal, for instance—a diamond will burn. A pure diamond will leave behind no ash. Carbon atoms will combine with oxygen and float off as gas, and the stone simply disappears.

Don't burn up diamonds. That was worth knowing.

Another key thing Arnold learned: it's incredibly easy to miss rough diamonds in nature. "Almost all gems conceal their beauties in a natural state," explained *Diamonds and Precious Stones: Their History, Value, and Distinguishing Characteristics*, published in 1865. When diamonds are expertly cut into elegant shapes with many flat edges, white light enters the gem, splits into the colors of the rainbow, and bounces out at different angles. Rough diamonds lack this fiery sparkle. "The diamond in the rough is most unattractive, and would be thrown away by a casual observer as a worthless pebble."

Don't throw diamonds away. Also good to know.

Two years of bookkeeping was more than enough for Arnold. Never an office guy to begin with, he bolted town to return to his true love—prospecting for riches in the American West.

Philip Arnold was no longer an ordinary miner, though. He now knew more about diamonds than almost anyone in the country.

In August 1871, Arnold sent a telegram from Reno, Nevada, to the diamond investors in San Francisco. Two months had passed since Arnold and Slack left town, promising to return with a hefty sample from their hidden mine. Now they were on their way back and wanted one of the investors to meet their train at Lathrop, California, seventy miles east of Frisco.

It was a good sign, Asbury Harpending and George Roberts agreed. The cousins must have hit pay dirt. Otherwise, why telegraph ahead?

Harpending hurried to Lathrop and waited on the platform. When the westbound train chugged in, he climbed aboard and strode down the aisles. In a car of well-dressed tourists and business travelers, the diamond hunters were easy to spot.

"Both were travel-strained and weather-beaten and had the general appearance of having gone through much hardship and privation," Harpending later wrote. "Slack was sound asleep like a tired-out man. Arnold sat grimly erect like a vigilant old soldier with a rifle by his side, also a bulky-looking buckskin package."

Harpending sat with the cousins. Slack woke up.

As the train rattled west, the miners told their story in lowered voices. They'd found their mine, all right. The ground was as rich as they'd first thought, richer maybe. They'd dug up a fortune in diamonds and other gems, then divided the stones into two big deerskin sacks. Each had carried one out of the wilderness.

They'd come to a high river, swollen with melting snow. They built a raft of logs and fought their way across, swept along by a raging current, nearly tossed overboard and drowned, and one of the bags slid into the whitewater and sank. There was no chance to recover it.

The other deerskin bag, stuffed with thirty-five pounds of gemstones?

That was sitting on the seat between them.

When the train reached Oakland, Harpending wrote a receipt for the package. It still belonged to the cousins, but they'd agreed to let Harpending borrow it for a while. He rode the ferry across the bay to San Francisco, a trip he'd made many times, though never with a bulky bundle that would make Aladdin burn with envy. Well, no one could possibly guess what was in the bag, right? That should keep him safe.

Hopping off the boat in Frisco, desperate to reach the comfort of home, Harpending was assailed with the usual barrage of newsboys waving papers and "hotel runners" competing for business.

"Russ House!" one roared. "Russ House!"

Others aggressively offered to take travelers to rival lodgings.

"Occidental Hotel!"

"Nucleus Hotel!"

Dodging the crowds, Harpending leapt into his own waiting carriage. His driver raced to the Harpending family mansion in the fashionable Rincon Hill neighborhood. George Roberts and three other potential diamond mine investors were already there.

Harpending jumped from the carriage and carried his bag inside.

8
DAZZLING LIGHT

The men hurried to Harpending's billiard room and shut the door. Harpending spread a sheet over the felt of his billiard table. He cut the sack open and tilted its top over the table. George Roberts and the others leaned forward.

Rough diamonds and rubies tumbled onto the sheet, clinking off each other, settling in piles on the fabric.

"It seemed," said Harpending, "like a dazzling, many-colored cataract of light."

The cascade of jewels did the trick. The investors were hooked.

William Lent, who'd been investing in mines for twenty years, examined individual stones for size and brilliancy. His only fear, he said, was that the mine might be *too* rich. What if they dug up so many diamonds, they actually drove diamond prices down?

George Sullivan Dodge, a Civil War general from Vermont, posed a more pressing question. "Where," he asked, "were the diamonds found?"

Unknown, Harpending explained. Slack and Arnold would only hint that the mine was in "Indian country." This likely meant somewhere in Arizona or New Mexico, where the cousins had often prospected before. Harpending told the group the story of Arnold and Slack nearly drowning in a flooded river and losing a package of jewels.

This absolutely amazed the investors. Had those two blockheads seriously left thirty-five pounds of diamonds at the bottom of a river? They must be mighty confident they could find more.

Dodge asked Harpending about Arnold, the clear leader of the two cousins.

"A peculiar man," Harpending said. "But have no fear, I can control him."

The others certainly hoped so. The gems on Harpending's

billiard table represented the find of a lifetime. Whoever controlled the mine was about to get very, very rich.

In the following days, Slack and Arnold bickered on the streets of San Francisco.

Slack had already sold half of his share of the diamond mine for $50,000. For another $50,000, he was willing to sell the rest to Harpending's group. A hundred grand, Slack told his cousin, was all he'd ever want in life.

Arnold urged Slack to hold out for more. The investors were wealthy, Arnold argued. And eager. And greedy as pigs. Why not demand half a million each, at the very least?

Slack wasn't tempted. Gaining legal control of the land, buying equipment, hiring crews to work and guard the mine—that was an expensive, long-term project. Slack had the chance to walk away a rich man right now, with no further effort or risk. Twenty-five years of prospecting was enough. He wanted out of the game.

Harpending's group happily paid Slack $50,000 in gold coins for the second half of his share of the diamond mine. Arnold could have taken the same deal.

He refused to sell at any price.

The investors figured they could deal with Arnold later. For now, they needed a plan of action. Harpending's crew included some of the biggest money men in San Francisco, but this diamond strike was too big for them to handle alone. They needed powerful lawyers—and political influence too. They had to make absolutely sure they secured legal control of the diamond field before anyone else knew it existed.

Harpending's team also wanted to hire their own mining engineer to assess the richness of the field. And they insisted on bringing a sample of the gems to New York City to get them appraised by the country's most famous jeweler, Charles Lewis Tiffany.

Arnold raised no objection to these proposals. He was pleased with the decision to consult Tiffany. "That will settle everything," he told Harpending.

All agreed that speed was essential. Thousands of miners were out there, scouring the mountains and streams and deserts of the West.

Asbury Harpending and his English pal Alfred Rubery, along with William Lent, General Dodge, and Philip Arnold, rode the transcontinental railroad east out of San Francisco. The train climbed through California's Sierra Nevada, sped across Nevada deserts and alongside Utah's Great Salt Lake. It chugged through the Rockies and on to the Great Plains, passing buffalo herds and fields of wildflowers, Plains Indians hunting on horseback, and homesteader cabins built from chunks of sod.

At small-town stops along the way, children stood outside restaurants clanging bells and calling out, "Meals! Meals for fifty cents!" The food, travelers commented, was always the same: beefsteak, fried eggs, fried potatoes. You had to check your watch to know if you were eating breakfast or supper.

The idea of a quick business trip to New York was shockingly new in 1871. The transcontinental railroad, connecting the East and West Coasts by rail, had been completed only two years before. The coast-to-coast journey by ship or ox-drawn wagon used to take months. Now, suddenly, it could be made in a week.

Life in America was changing fast. And no one knew where things were headed.

Congress had just passed the Indian Appropriations Act of 1871, declaring that the government no longer recognized Indian tribes as sovereign nations. The government had long used threats and violence to pressure Native American leaders into signing land treaties that favored the United States. With the new law, there would be no more negotiation—the government would simply seize the land it wanted and use the military to drive Indians onto reservations. Native American nations put up determined resistance, leading to wars across the West in the years to come.

The country was also in the midst of Reconstruction, the stormy years after the Civil War. President Ulysses S. Grant's government was struggling to bring the former Confederate states back into the Union, and to extend rights to four million Black citizens who had been enslaved. The Fifteenth Amendment, ratified in 1870, guaranteed voting rights for Black men. For the first time in American history, Black leaders won election to the U.S. House and Senate, all from Southern states. Former Confederate leaders and racist terrorist groups fought this progress, often violently. The Fourteenth Amendment, ratified in 1868, guaranteed equal protection of the law to all American citizens—but when would that become a reality?

At the same time, Elizabeth Cady Stanton and Susan B. Anthony helped lead the growing women's suffrage movement, pressing for an amendment to the Constitution granting women the right to vote. American women had full voting rights only in Wyoming Territory, which passed a voting rights law in 1869, and Utah Territory, which followed in 1870. Not a single state allowed women to vote in statewide or national elections—and women were determined to correct this injustice.

In October 1871, as Harpending's group crossed the country, a massive fire tore through the city of Chicago, killing about three hundred people, destroying seventeen thousand buildings, and leaving one-third of the city's residents homeless. The same night the Great Chicago Fire started, a less famous but far deadlier blaze roared out of the forests of northeast Wisconsin, ripping through the town of Peshtigo and surrounding areas.

The Peshtigo fire killed at least fifteen hundred people, making it the most devastating fire in American history.

Amid all this news and turbulence, no one noticed a small group of investors from California step off the train in New York City. Asbury Harpending braced for the challenge of a lifetime. Sixteen years before, he'd gone west with five bucks in his pocket. Now, at thirty-two, he arrived in the nation's biggest city, the financial center of America's booming economy. As always, he was brimming with confidence. He'd faced his share of upheaval and risk. Whatever was coming his way, Harpending was sure he could handle it.

9

THE GILDED AGE

Philip Arnold must have felt very far from home.

He'd lived in Frisco, sure, but New York was nearly ten times the size—taller buildings, busier shops and sidewalks, elevated trains rumbling above traffic-filled streets. In the East River between Manhattan and Brooklyn, hundreds of workers had begun building the Brooklyn Bridge, the longest suspension bridge ever attempted.

This was the start of the Gilded Age, a time of rapid economic growth that saw the United States pass European rivals to become the world's greatest industrial power. A small handful of super-wealthy men took control of key industries: oil, steel, banking, mining, railroads—even government. The era was infamous for political corruption, with (some, not all) elected leaders grabbing cash in exchange for making laws favorable to big business.

Arnold walked smack into the Gilded Age. As soon as

he arrived in New York, Harpending and the other investors dragged him to a glittering four-story mansion on Madison Avenue. This was the home of Samuel Barlow, a rich lawyer with powerful connections in business and politics. Barlow had agreed to represent the diamond investors.

In addition to the diamond team, Barlow invited a few of the city's elite movers and shakers. The jeweler Charles Lewis Tiffany was there to assess the value of Arnold's gems. General George McClellan, commander of the Union army during the Civil War and a former presidential candidate, joined the group in Barlow's study. So did Horace Greeley, a newspaper publisher and one of the country's most famous people. A few Wall Street bankers gathered around as well, hoping to get in on the diamond mine before news of its discovery got out.

Harpending, in a repeat of the dramatic scene in his billiard room back home, opened his bag of jewels and let the stones tumble free.

Tiffany leaned forward, sorting them, holding one after another to the flame of a gas lamp. The man knew what he was doing, Harpending thought. Everyone enjoyed the show.

Finally, with theatrical flair, Tiffany addressed his audience. "Gentlemen, these are beyond question precious stones of enormous value."

How enormous, precisely?

"I cannot fix an exact value," Tiffany said. He offered to take the gems to his shop and have his expert staff take a look.

Tiffany made his report two days later. He valued the gems in Harpending's bag at $150,000. This was fantastic news. Harpending had brought only one-tenth of the jewels from Arnold and Slack's original package. So that one package alone must be worth $1.5 million! More than enough to justify paying Arnold almost any price for his share of the mine.

Another key objective, to put it bluntly, was to bribe a member of Congress.

Samuel Barlow explained this to his clients. It was essential to gain legal control of the land on which the diamond mine was located. To do this, they'd need to make a small change to the country's mining laws—existing laws about claiming land covered precious metals, but not gemstones. Until now, no one thought there *were* diamond deposits in North America. Did this sound terribly complicated? Not to worry, Barlow said. He'd handle everything.

The lawyer added Benjamin Butler, a member of the House of Representatives from Massachusetts, to his legal staff. Yes, this was the whiskered congressman for whom a giant sea lion in San Francisco Bay was named. Ben Butler was a classic example of human complexity: an outspoken champion of civil rights for Black Americans—who at the same time was perfectly willing to take money to rewrite laws for rich pals.

The investors also needed to hire a mining engineer to visit the site and make sure it was as rich as Slack and Arnold claimed. Barlow suggested Henry Janin. One of the country's top engineers, Janin had inspected hundreds of gold and silver mines. He was known to be very careful and accurate.

"The O.K. of Henry Janin fixed the reputation of a mining property in every market," Harpending noted with approval.

As a fee, Janin wanted $2,500 cash, plus the right to buy a thousand shares of stock in the investors' diamond company—once it was formed—for just $10 each. If the mine proved to be rich, Janin knew, the stock would make him wealthy.

Philip Arnold appeared to be getting nervous. Could he trust any of these slick Yankees? The high-priced lawyer, the congressman, the mining engineer—they were all working for the other guys, the ones trying to buy him out. Who was looking out for him?

"Suppose I go in the spring," Arnold asked, referring to his secret site, "and the man they select says the ground is not what I have represented?"

A fair point. Arnold could lead Henry Janin to the mine only to have the engineer declare it worth less than Arnold had estimated. What if Janin was wrong? Or what if he purposely undervalued the mine to trick Arnold into selling too cheap?

"You might trust these men if you want to, but I will not," Arnold told Harpending. "I will not sign any paper unless I have a payment on my share."

A payment? This was the first time Arnold expressed a willingness to sell. Harpending leapt at the opportunity.

He dragged Arnold back to Barlow's office, where they hammered out a deal. Arnold agreed to sell half his share of the mine; he absolutely refused to part with all of it. He agreed to lead Henry Janin to the site. In exchange, Harpending and the other investors would pay Arnold $100,000 now, and an additional $150,000 if Janin's report was satisfactory.

After signing the contracts, Arnold undid the top few buttons of his shirt. Grabbing his stacks of cash, he lined them around his stomach and buttoned back up.

It was already too late in the year to lead an expedition into the snowy mountains of the West. Everyone agreed to meet up again in the spring, when Arnold would guide a group, including Harpending and Janin, to the site of his hidden mine. With the modern equivalent of about $2.6 million stuffed in his shirt, Arnold's business in New York was complete. He announced that he needed a vacation and was going to Kansas to enjoy some buffalo hunting.

He did not go to Kansas.

10

LONG WINTER

Back in San Francisco, poor George Roberts was no better off than when this story began.

It was a year since the night Arnold and Slack walked into his office, spilling stones on his desk, setting his heart racing. This was supposed to be the big strike that would save his bacon. "I am depending on the A. matter to bring us out," Roberts wrote to Harpending.

And maybe this *would* prove to be the jackpot of his dreams. But for now, Roberts was out even more money. When would some cash start coming in? As fall turned to winter, he was more jittery than ever.

"Money is tight," Roberts confided to Harpending, who was spending the winter in London, "and I am in much need of it."

Roberts still had no idea where the diamond mine was, and he was totally dependent on Philip Arnold. He'd feel a lot better if he could talk to Arnold—but no one knew where the man was. Roberts went often to see Mary Arnold, asking for updates on her husband. She had none.

"Mrs. A. has not heard from him since he left," Roberts told Harpending.

Yes, Mary Arnold was back in Frisco with her kids. She and Phil had patched things up, she told Roberts. Where was her husband? She didn't know—he often disappeared for months at a time. Hadn't he said something about hunting buffalo? Samuel Barlow, the investors' lawyer in New York, hired a Kansas City private eye to track Arnold down. The detective found no trace of Arnold in the Midwest.

By early 1872, Roberts feared the worst. Had Arnold hornswoggled him? Taken his cash and disappeared, never to reveal the location of his fabulous mine?

* * *

Asbury Harpending was in as deep as Roberts, but worrying just wasn't his style. He spent a few months with his wife and children at Morley's Hotel in London's upscale Trafalgar Square, racking up bills for ale and brandy and boarding fees for his servants.

Finally, on March 18, 1872, good news arrived from Roberts. "Mr. Arnold arrived here," Harpending read. "A. appears impatient to make his contemplated trip soon and inquired particularly about your movements."

Blank No. 7.

THE WESTERN UNION TELEGRAPH COMPANY.

THOS. T KOKERT. Gen'l Sup't.
New York

WILLIAM ORTON Pre't.
O.H. PALMER. Sec'y.
New York

Dated March 18 1872:

Received at London

To A. Harpending

Mr. Arnold arrived here.
A. appears impatient to make
his contemplated trip soon and
inquired particularly about your
movements.

As Harpending prepared to sail back to America, more good news arrived—President Grant had signed the Mining Law of 1872. The purpose of the law was to clarify rules about how citizens could claim rights to gold and other precious metals found on government land. Thanks to Representative Benjamin Butler, the law also allowed citizens to claim "valuable mineral deposits" such as diamonds. No one thought much of it at the time.

And no one knew, until later, that Butler had accepted one thousand shares of diamond mine stock in exchange for his little addition to the law.

On June 1, 1872, six men dressed for outdoor adventure stepped off the train at the tiny station of Rawlins in Wyoming Territory. The group was led by Philip Arnold and John Slack. Asbury Harpending was there, along with Alfred Rubery, fellow investor George S. Dodge, and Henry Janin, the mining expert.

Riding horses, leading mules packed high with food and water, blankets, tents, and hunting rifles, the group rode south from the railroad into the high desert. This was the northern edge of the traditional land of the Ute Indians, a sunbaked, rugged country of buttes and shrubs, yellow-green grass and reddish-brown dirt.

Harpending still thought the diamond mine was somewhere in the Southwest—Arizona or New Mexico. That's what Arnold and Slack had been hinting all along. So why were they starting out from Wyoming?

Were they seriously going to ride five hundred miles?

PART 3

BEYOND CALCULATION

Arnold and Slack led a winding march through southern Wyoming.
"The country was wild and inhospitable," Asbury Harpending would later recall.
Henry Janin, the country's top mining engineer, studied the region's geology as the group rode south.

"At times our leaders seemed to be perplexed," Harpending remembered.

In other words, they were lost.

Finally, late on the fourth day:
This is it.

The men began searching right away.

FWISH
TANG

Yeeehaaahhh!

Come, Rubery, is that honest now?

That's a diamond, any fool can see as much.

11

HAPPY MOOD

Henry Janin confirmed it—the stone in Rubery's hand was a real diamond. Hooting with excitement, the men spread out and searched, hacking at the hard ground as the sun sank below arid hills.

"We began to have all kinds of luck," Asbury Harpending recalled of his first day at the mine. "I had not been on the ground three minutes before I found a large diamond."

He looked over at Janin, who had become "wildly enthusiastic." The famously cautious engineer was scrambling over rocks, plucking jewels from the ground like a kid in a dream.

Arnold and Slack were helpful, the others noted. Rather than hunting diamonds themselves, they spent their time pointing out the richest spots, places where they'd had the best success. Before dark, all the investors found diamonds. Rubies too.

"You may depend upon it that we were in a happy mood

that night," said Harpending. "There wasn't the usual row over who should cook supper, who should wash the dishes."

Harpending and the others had harbored high hopes for this diamond field. What they'd just experienced went far beyond their greediest dreams. As they gathered around the campfire, Harpending, Dodge, and Rubery were tipsy with the thrill of sudden wealth. Janin went on and on about the honor of having his name forever linked to "the most momentous discovery of the age." Arnold and Slack were tired but satisfied.

At one point, during a lull in the conversation, the faint wail of a whistle drifted across the plateau. Must be a train, Harpending suggested.

Arnold smiled at the absurdity of this. The railroad, he assured Harpending, was at least a hundred miles away.

Sunrise gave the miners a glorious view of their diamond mine.

The field sat atop a rocky mesa—a flat-topped hill with steep sides. Crevasses crisscrossed the tan sandstone. Pebbles and reddish dirt lay in patches on the flat surface. To the south rose a lone mountain, Diamond Peak as it became known, its slopes covered with dark green pines. In all other directions, the landscape was wide open: dry hills to the horizon, sagebrush and small trees, an enormous blue sky.

Henry Janin took the lead as they got back to work, instructing the men to dig up dirt and carry it down to a creek below the plateau. Kneeling in the shallow water, Janin used a gold mining pan to wash the dirt. He swirled water in the pan, causing light sand to spill over the edge, leaving heavier stones behind. Some were diamonds. It was a slow process. Arnold stuck by Janin's side, helping with the tedious labor.

"Two days' work satisfied Janin of the absolute genuineness of the diamond fields," Harpending recalled.

What next? Harpending and Janin disagreed. Janin wanted to spend a week trying to figure out how extensive the diamond field actually was. Harpending wanted to head home. Their mission was accomplished, he argued. They'd come to inspect the field, and that was done. The priority now was to begin the process of legally claiming the land and forming a company to work the mine. The other men, with sore backs and blistered hands, sided with Harpending.

As a compromise, the group spent a few days hammering

wooden stakes into the ground, attaching handwritten signs claiming control of the land and streams and nearby pine forests. "We staked off in a rough way an enormous stretch of the country," Harpending recalled, "what we believed to be the entire diamondiferous area."

Yes, *diamondiferous* is a real word. And no, the handwritten signs had no legal value. But might they at least scare away a stray miner who wandered onto the field? It was worth a try.

As the men packed their mules, Harpending had another worry: Were they really going to leave this world-changing bonanza just lying there unguarded?

John Slack volunteered to stay and stand guard. Harpending was grateful and asked Rubery to stay behind as well. "This Rubery rebelled against lustily," Harpending said. "He had come on a pleasure trip—nothing more." Also, Rubery hated Slack, looking down on the miner as a crude clodhopper. Slack returned the hostility, seeing Rubery as a citified dandy, soft and useless. Harpending had to promise Rubery $300 a week to get him to stay.

Arnold led Harpending, Janin, and Dodge back through southern Wyoming—taking a different meandering route to a different station on the transcontinental railroad. They bought tickets for New York and headed east. From Laramie, Wyoming,

Harpending telegraphed William Ralston, the San Francisco banker, with this key update:

Blank No. 7.

THE WESTERN UNION TELEGRAPH COMPANY.

THOS. T KOKERT. Gen'l Sup't. New York

WILLIAM ORTON Pre't. O.H. PALMER. Sec'y. New York

Dated June 18 1872:

Received at San Francisco

To W. Ralston

four and five in great quantities

Any guesses at the meaning? Is the *four* "diamonds" and the *five* "rubies"?

Harpending used a cipher because he knew messages sent by telegraph were never really private. To send a telegram, you'd write out your note and hand it to an operator, who then turned your words into the dots and dashes of Morse code and sent the message as electrical pulses along wires. This technology revolutionized the speed of communication—but operators sending and receiving messages were sometimes tempted to sell bits of juicy news. Like the discovery of a rich new mine, for example.

To create his ciphers, Harpending made lists of words, names, and phrases he might need to use. He then assigned a code word or phrase to each one. It's a simple system used by spies throughout history. You basically create your own coded dictionary—and make sure to share it with only your most trusted associates. Here are a few samples from one of the handwritten lists found in Harpending's business records:

Code Word/Phrase	Meaning
Sugar	Diamonds
Salt	Rubies
Spoons	Shovels
Burk	Arnold
Fairfax	Roberts
We are all well	We are all pleased with the mines. Fully sustain reports.
Send us the papers	Mine is not satisfactory.
Will stop at Salt Lake	Have abandoned the trip.
Send my luggage by express	Will meet you on arrival of cars, but don't recognize me. Follow the direction I go and horses will be ready to mount as soon as we get to camp.

That last one is oddly specific, but it must have come in handy at some point. It's the system of a man obsessed with secrecy and sneaky movement. The sort of thing that would later make people wonder about Harpending's exact role in these events.

For now, everyone was happy. Harpending continued to New York City in high spirits.

Rubery and Slack lasted only two days at the diamond field they were meant to be guarding. There are no good sources for the nasty barbs the enemies exchanged while standing watch on that windy mesa. It's too bad! Rubery would only say, without offering details, that he and Slack "quarreled very severely."

Unable to bear each other's company a moment longer, Rubery trekked north to the railroad. Slack rode east from the field, walking away with his $100,000 profit.

He was not seen again by anyone in this story.

12

WILD SCRAMBLE

Henry Janin's report on his trip to the diamond field struck New York like lightning.

As an engineer, Janin was famous for his safe, conservative estimates of the value of mines. It was not his job to get excited. Still, you can almost *feel* the excitement bursting through his carefully chosen words.

"While I did not have time enough to make the investigations which would have answered very important questions," Janin reported, "I do not doubt that further prospecting will result in finding diamonds over a greater area than is as yet proved to be diamond-bearing."

Then there was this:

"In conclusion, I would say that I consider this a wonderfully rich discovery, and one that will prove extremely profitable."

Wonderfully rich. Extremely profitable. These phrases—coming from Henry Janin—made investors drool. All of a sudden, the country caught what newspapers began to call "diamond fever."

"There was a wild scramble to get on board," Asbury Harpending recalled, "almost at any price."

Diamond fever jumped the ocean to Europe. Baron Lionel de Rothschild, a British politician and one of the world's richest bankers, contacted Harpending by transatlantic cable to get confirmation of the diamond discovery.

"I answered Baron Rothschild that half the truth had not been told," Harpending later reported. "That the diamond fields were rich beyond calculation; that every doubt and shadow of a doubt had been absolutely removed."

Rothschild believed it. Why not? "America is a rich land," he said. "It has given us many surprises. It reserves many more."

The only one upset by the spread of diamond fever was Philip Arnold.

By agreement, Arnold was due $150,000 for Janin's confirmation of the richness of his mine, plus more for his remaining share of the find. But now, Arnold complained, that was looking like a lousy deal. The mine was so much richer than even *he* had expected. He'd sold out way too cheap!

"If I only had the property back in my hands," Arnold ranted and raved, "I would tell you all to go to the devil."

This was a critical moment for Harpending and his partners. They'd poured everything into this project—money and time and dreams of an empire of jewels. The thought of Arnold walking away now, with a big portion of the mine still under his control, was terrifying.

"Have no fear," Harpending had once said of Arnold. "I can control him."

He set out to do just that, inviting Arnold to stay at a riverfront home he rented north of the city. Looking out at spectacular views of the Hudson River, with green hills rising above the wide stretch of water, Harpending worked his charms. Eventually, he succeeded in persuading Arnold to honor their agreement.

Still grumbling at the unfairness of it all, Arnold accepted his $150,000, plus another $300,000 for his remaining share of the mine.

"Thus, the decks were cleared," Harpending crowed.

Asbury Harpending was the hero of the hour. Thanks to his brilliant maneuvers, the team from San Francisco had gotten rid of the two pesky cousins once and for all. The mine had cost them $650,000, but so what? For the richest diamond find in the history of the world, it was the bargain of the century!

There was only one problem. A fairly important detail, you might say.

The diamond mine did not exist.

13

DIAMONDS AND SALT

To put it more precisely, there *were* diamonds buried in the land Harpending and friends had just purchased. But nature had not put them there.

The idea of creating a fake mine was nothing new. This type of crime was known as "salting"—a common scam in the West. Shady miners, for instance, had been known to salt streams by scattering real gold in the water. Or they shaved pieces off gold coins, loaded the slivers into shotgun shells, and blasted bits of yellow metal into rocks. They could then "discover" the gold-bearing stone and sell the site for a handsome profit.

One extreme version of salting relied on a product named the "Gold Cure," a so-called medicine that claimed to treat alcoholism. The doctor selling this elixir said his secret formula included real gold, which would "disinfect the blood," according to his advertisement, "leaving the patient sound and healthy, giving a remarkable increase in nerve, power, vigor and strength."

Salters saw another use for this snake oil. Why not drink it—and then urinate detectable amounts of precious metal into cracks between rocks?

The perfect way to fake a gold mine? Not really. To save a few bucks, the doctor who peddled this miracle cure had actually stopped using real gold in his formula. He kept the word *gold* in the name as a marketing ploy.

Philip Arnold and John Slack knew these sorts of stories. They knew that anyone who'd been around the mining world of the West was wary of salting scams. This, they figured, could work to their advantage. People would be wary of hoaxes, sure—but not with diamonds. Diamonds were too rare, too valuable to use in this way. If a person could afford to buy bags full of diamonds, why would they need to pull a scam for money?

This was the brilliantly simple idea behind what would go down in history as the Great Diamond Hoax.

* * *

If you want to scam someone (and I'm not recommending it), here's the first rule:

Figure out what the person wants to hear—and tell it to them.

Okay, now let's go back to where the story began. Back to the night in San Francisco when Arnold and Slack showed up in Roberts's office with a bag of rough diamonds. George Roberts was desperate for a big score, right? Roberts wanted to hear that he could get in on a rich mining strike, something no one else knew about. So this is where the cousins decided to start. They made Roberts promise to keep their discovery secret—but they knew he could never do it.

Roberts took the stones to a jeweler, exactly as the cousins had hoped. They knew the stones were real. Arnold had bought (or possibly stolen) the diamonds from the drill company where he'd worked as a bookkeeper. That little bag he and Slack brought to Roberts's office wasn't enough to salt a diamond mine—but it *was* enough to get Roberts and his friends excited. The cousins acted as if they didn't want to sell. All part of the plan. Finally, Roberts and Harpending "persuaded" Slack to take $50,000 for half his share of the mine.

Now the cousins had enough money to salt a diamond mine.

They also used the cash George Roberts paid directly to Mary Arnold, the $20,000 that Roberts owed Phil Arnold from a previous deal. Remember how Phil and Mary had fought over this money? Mary demanded it be paid directly to her—and she got it. It would later become clear that she and Phil had staged their stormy breakup. After leaving Frisco with the twenty grand, Mary met Phil in St. Louis and handed over the money.

Arnold and Slack continued by railroad to New York and hopped on a steamship to London. Slack traveled under his middle name, Burchem. Arnold went by the name of Aundle.

They were better at plotting crimes than inventing fake names.

A London jeweler would never forget their visit to his shop that summer. The two strangers were roughly dressed and spoke in harsh American accents. They pawed through trays of uncut diamonds and rubies, setting aside huge piles for purchase, showing no interest at all in the weight or quality of individual stones.

How did they plan to pay? the jeweler inquired.

The chap called Aundle whipped out a roll of bills and blurted, "How much for the lot?"

The cousins then steamed back across the Atlantic and rode the train to California. Fast travel was key to their clever deception. Just a couple of years before, the six-thousand-mile trip from London to Frisco would have taken several months. Now, thanks to modern steamships and the new transcontinental railroad, they could make the trip in under three weeks. This was so new that no one really considered it. The cousins simply were not gone long enough for anyone to imagine they'd been to another continent.

Arnold and Slack handed Harpending the thirty-five-pound

bag of gems and a thrilling tale of having lost a second bag in a flooded river. The investors headed to New York City, where Charles Lewis Tiffany, the country's foremost jeweler, declared Arnold's rough jewels to be "beyond question precious stones of enormous value."

They weren't, though.

The stones were not *worthless*—the cousins paid good money for them in London. But neither Tiffany nor his "expert" staff knew how to value uncut gems. Tiffany declared the bag of stones to be worth $150,000.

In fact, it was worth one-tenth of that.

Why didn't Tiffany just admit he didn't know what he was talking about? People rarely do. Slack and Arnold were counting on this.

After getting his first payment—the cash he stuffed into his shirt—Arnold told Harpending he was off to Kansas to hunt. In fact, he made another buying trip to Europe, departing from Canada to avoid being seen by anyone he knew, and returning with another load of rough gemstones. He met Slack somewhere along the western railroad.

Now all they had to do was create a diamond mine.

Where? The cousins already had an ideal spot in mind.

The mine needed to be remote, isolated enough so that no one would stumble onto it by chance. Not *too* isolated, though.

It had to be somewhat near a railroad line so that they could get in and out fairly quickly. And the land had to look right. Arnold was no geologist, but he'd done a fair amount of reading at the drill company in San Francisco. He had a basic idea of what the diamond-rich regions of Brazil and South Africa looked like.

The cousins zeroed in on a lonely stretch of high desert in the northwest corner of Colorado, along the border of Wyoming, about 7,500 feet above sea level.

Arnold and Slack most likely made several trips to the site. One was certainly in early 1872, while Arnold was supposedly hunting buffalo in Kansas. The cousins hacked hundreds of holes in the hard earth and buried diamonds all over the mesa. They dropped jewels into cracks in the rocky surface, using long sticks to drive them deeper underground.

With this new information in mind, let's replay the scene of Arnold wailing to the investors in New York City:

It was a performance worthy of the new theaters opening on a New York avenue called Broadway. The audience was completely taken in.

Philip Arnold must have laughed all the way back to Frisco. His total take from the Great Diamond Hoax was $550,000—$15 million in today's money. All from an investment, with John Slack, of about $50,000.

When Phil got to California, he and Mary packed up the house they'd lived in for the past three years. Arnold would later point out that this was done openly—they even advertised their furniture in the newspaper. The Arnolds did not, as was suggested, slink from the city under cover of night.

Philip and Mary, along with their children, headed home to Elizabethtown, Kentucky. They bought a redbrick mansion near town, a huge home with marble fireplaces, crystal chandeliers, and a very big safe. Phil purchased a new headstone for his mother's grave.

And Philip Arnold settled into the quiet life of a country gentleman. It was fun.

But not fun enough.

14

THE WILD EAST

That summer, while walking his beat near the White House, a Washington police officer named William West spotted a two-horse carriage speeding down 13th Street. Literally speeding. West jumped into the road, signaling with his club for the driver to stop.

Only when the carriage pulled over did West see that the driver was Ulysses S. Grant. The president of the United States was known to race friends through town, posing a danger to pedestrians. West let Grant off with a warning.

The next evening Grant sped down the street again, this time racing a pack of other buggies. Again, West waved his club. Grant tugged the reins of his carriage, bringing his horses to a stop.

As West walked up to Grant, he saw a bashful smile on the president's face. Like a schoolboy caught making mischief by his teacher, West thought.

Grant asked, "Do you think, officer, that I was violating the speed laws?"

"I do, Mr. President," West said.

"Well, what do you want me to do?"

West reminded Grant that he'd been warned the day before. "I am very sorry, Mr. President, to have to do it, for you are the chief of the nation, and I am nothing but a policeman, but duty is duty, sir, and I will have to place you under arrest."

This was the first time an American president had ever been arrested. Grant was taken to the police station and forced to fork over a $20 fine. The president's friends objected on his behalf. They even tried to get West fired. West, who'd been born into slavery in Maryland and fought for the Union in the Civil War, was one of only two Black police officers in the entire city.

Grant backed the lawman. He even sent a personal note to the chief of police commending William West for doing his duty.

Maybe the most amazing thing about this story is that it didn't leak to the press. Washington had many competing newspapers, and they all loved tales of true crime and celebrity scandal. Grant must have been grateful; he was running for reelection and had already been chosen as the Republican Party candidate. For his opponent, Democrats picked Horace Greeley—the famous newspaper publisher who'd been in Samuel Barlow's New York mansion when the jeweler Tiffany declared Harpending's bag of diamonds "beyond question precious stones of enormous value."

The Grant-Greeley showdown was, of course, a big story all through the summer of 1872.

So was the ongoing drama of a stupendous diamond strike somewhere out West. Excitement over the discovery of diamonds, reported the *San Francisco Chronicle*, "has already become intense and is hourly increasing."

15
CALIFORNIA STREET

It was tough to get much work done in the offices of Asbury Harpending's brand-new San Francisco and New York Mining and Commercial Company.

More than a thousand people lined up outside company headquarters on Frisco's Market Street. Crowds snaked through the office all day, waiting their turn to glimpse a display case full of diamonds. This company had made what looked like the biggest strike of any kind in the history of the West—and there was the proof, for all to see, inside the showcase.

"Many enthusiastic expressions were heard," noted a local reporter. Harpending mingled with visitors, proudly informing folks the stones were from "his" diamond fields.

And he was right. Harpending and his partners George Roberts, William Ralston, and William Lent held most of the company's hundred thousand shares of stock, valued at $100 each. Stacks of letters arrived every day with requests to buy shares. The company had to hire a crew of clerks to keep up with the mail. But, at this point, the stock was not available to the public—only to a few select people who could make the company even more powerful. General George McClellan invested. The Rothschild banking family bought in.

Harpending, Roberts, and friends had no intention of selling their own shares until the price went higher.

Much higher.

Well, if ordinary folks couldn't invest, they could at least come see the stones that had sparked the country's diamond fever. They could gape longingly at a map on the office wall showing the three thousand acres Henry Janin staked out that summer, with spots tantalizingly labeled Diamond Peak, Diamond Flat, Ruby Gulch—and Arnold Creek.

Where were these magical-sounding places? The map offered no clue. No nearby geographic features were labeled. You couldn't even tell what state or territory you were looking at.

"On California Street scarcely anything else was talked of," reported a *San Francisco Chronicle* writer who hung around the city's financial center for a couple of days.

Asked for his opinion on Harpending's company, one broker told the reporter: "It is either the grandest discovery ever made in mining or it is the biggest job that was ever put up."

The biggest scam, in other words.

"There is no doubt," the reporter pointed out, "that they have a large lot of genuine diamonds here, at any rate."

"No; there can be no doubt of that. But where did they come from?"

Was the broker questioning Harpending's story?

Not exactly. But he was wary. "It is too rich," he said, "too good to be true."

"It is too big a story," another broker chimed in as he hurried past. "Sounds too much like a fairy tale. I don't want any. I ain't on it. Good day."

But most believed in the mine's rich promise, largely because of the people behind the venture—respected bankers, lawyers, political leaders.

"I can't believe these are the kind of men to make up such a thing," an insurance company president told the reporter. "I don't believe they would dare to do it, for it would ruin them when the truth comes out."

This was a commonly heard argument. Harpending's reputation was shaky, thanks in part to the whole Confederate pirate thing. But now he was a respected citizen of San Francisco, owner of valuable buildings in the city. He simply had too much to lose. Trust in the word of Henry Janin went a long way too.

"You bet, I have got the stock, and I have paid my money for it," Janin told a broker.

He and the other investors were poised to make millions. And yet no one other than Slack and Arnold had yet seen a dime. In fact, Harpending and George Roberts were out hundreds of thousands of dollars. They planned to put their stock up for sale—at the right moment—and walk away with life-changing fortunes.

But not yet, for one key reason. They still did not have legal control of the diamond field.

To finalize their claim, the diamond company first had to send out a party to conduct an official survey of the land—this was part of the legal process. What if someone else found the field before this survey was done? There'd be nothing to stop them from digging up the diamonds. Harpending and Roberts would be ruined.

Which made the location of their diamond field the most valuable secret on earth.

So, of course, everyone tried to solve the puzzle.

"No, there is nothing more that I feel inclined to state just yet," George Roberts told a reporter. "People are anxious to know the locality, and I suppose I have been asked where it is a thousand times today."

Other company officials were equally cagey. When asked for a clue to the mine's location, one said: "About 1,000 miles to the east of Ralston's office."

Did that mean directly east? Northeast? Southeast? And exactly how many miles were "about 1,000"? These vague directions could lead seekers to Colorado, Wyoming, New Mexico, Arizona, or maybe even Utah or Idaho.

In private, the diamond company officers were not quite so calm. Competing teams in towns all over the West were gearing up to search for the mine. Harpending's company *had* to get there first with their survey crew.

Besides, weren't Slack and Rubery still out there guarding the site? Poor fellows must be running short of grub by now.

The situation was tricky. Harpending and the other top investors were literally watched night and day for clues. Any expedition leaving from the city was sure to be followed. And there was another big problem—sort of embarrassing, given the enormous fortunes at stake: None of the investors knew how to get to their mine. They'd been there, sure, but Arnold had led them on such a long and grueling trek through a vast, remote region . . . Could they really be certain of finding it again?

The diamond company was in desperate need of help. They were in desperate need of Philip Arnold.

16

THE COUNTRY GENTLEMAN

And, in a way, Philip Arnold needed the diamond company.

He needed *something*, anyway.

Sporting a fine suit, chomping on a toothpick, Arnold swaggered around the little town where he'd once been a lowly hatter's apprentice. He enjoyed being the center of attention but just wasn't cut out to be a country gentleman. What had seemed like the ultimate goal proved to be pretty dull.

We can only imagine Arnold's surprise when a telegram arrived from the San Francisco and New York Mining and Commercial Company. They wanted him to lead a group of surveyors back to the diamond mine.

Why would he even consider doing this?

He'd just pulled off one of the greatest scams in American history. He'd cashed in and made it safely home, a rich man for life. No one suspected him. He'd done a masterful job of confusing the investors about the mine's location, convincing them it was over a hundred miles from the railroad when it was actually closer to forty. So why return to the scene of the crime?

Well, there was some practical benefit to staying involved. The diamond field was real as far as Arnold knew, right? So why not stick around? Why not be helpful? Then he could act as surprised as anyone when the mine turned out to be fake. After all, if he were really guilty of salting the mine himself, wouldn't he stay as far away as possible?

That's one argument. For Arnold, the thrill of the game was an even bigger draw. He'd had the time of his life playing that diamond-hunting bumpkin, toying with elite money men on two coasts. He wanted the game to continue. It's a classic feature of history's great scam artists—they simply can't walk away from their creations.

Do they want to be caught?

Do they need people to know all about the brilliant thing they've done?

Are they simply having too much fun to quit while they're ahead?

For whatever reason, or combination of reasons, Arnold took the job. Of course he knew it was only a matter of time before everything exploded. For now, the investors were totally fooled. The immediate danger was that someone else could find the mine and expose the hoax.

The West was a mighty big place, though. Was anyone really lucky enough—or smart enough—to locate that remote and lonely plateau?

PART 4

GEOLOGIST IN CHARGE

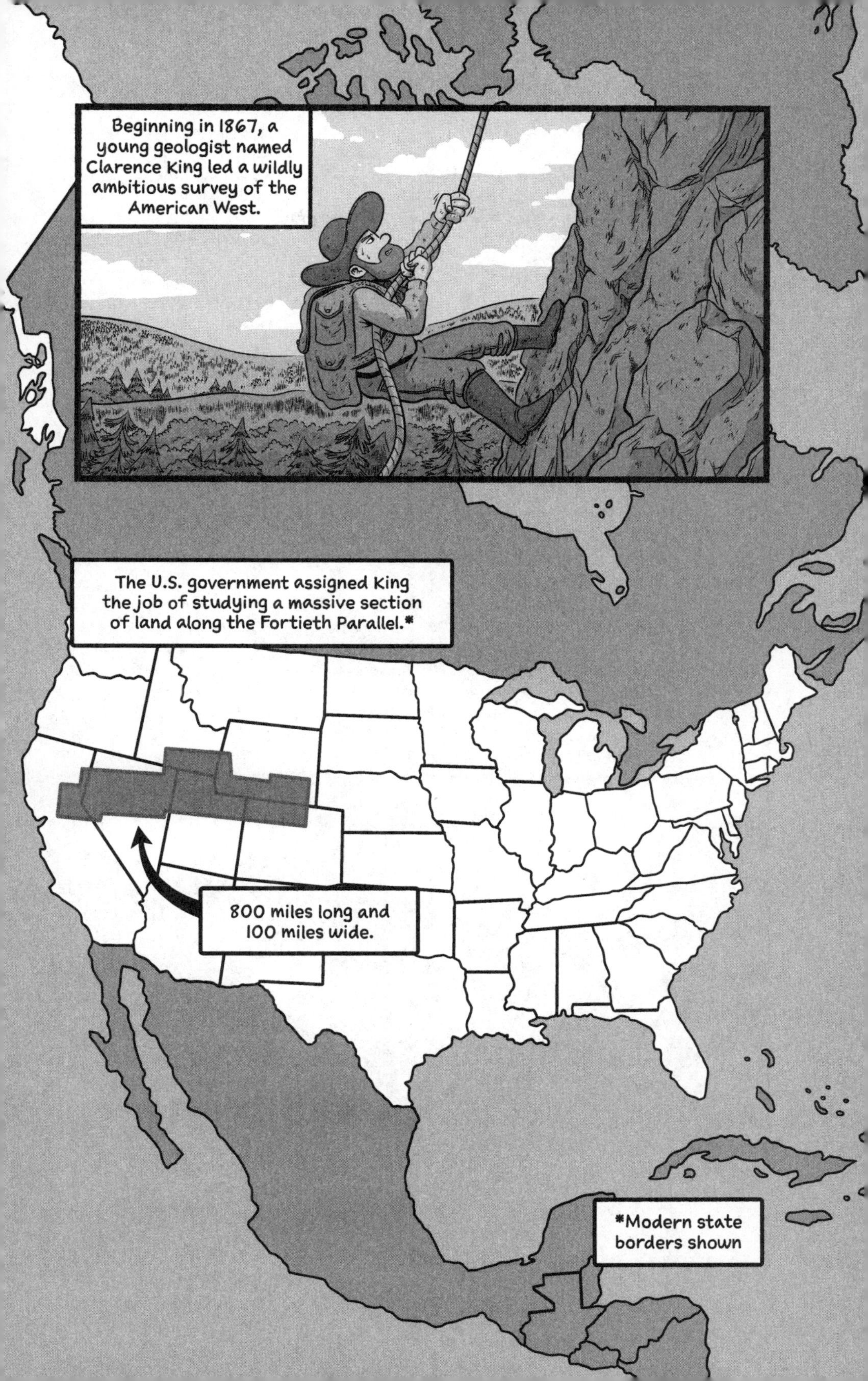
Beginning in 1867, a young geologist named Clarence King led a wildly ambitious survey of the American West.
The U.S. government assigned King the job of studying a massive section of land along the Fortieth Parallel.*
800 miles long and 100 miles wide.
*Modern state borders shown

King was endlessly thrilled by the wonders of nature.

HA HA!!

GREAT JONES!

For five years, the crew drew detailed maps, took photographs, and studied the natural history and mineral resources of the West.

The work required hauling equipment up slopes mules couldn't travel.

Using barometers, they calculated the height of some of the tallest mountains in the country.

Barometers measure air pressure—essentially the weight of the air above you. This pressure decreases as you get higher above sea level.

The work was difficult—and very dangerous.
"I was staggered," King wrote of the lightning strike, "and my brain and nerves severely shocked."
But he was soon back on the trail.
One of the young surveyor members, Samuel Emmons, said:
With him nothing was impossible that was worth doing. His enthusiasm was so contagious.
King once insisted on sliding down a snowy mountain—with no sled.
A botanist named William Brewer said:
He came out of the adventure with only a few unimportant bruises.

The year 1872 was the sixth and final year of King's epic Fortieth Parallel Survey.
By remarkable coincidence, the King survey included the exact spot that Arnold and Slack chose for their diamond mine.

17

CLARENCE KING

"For me the study or the laboratory would have been utterly impossible," Clarence King once said.

From a young age, King knew he needed to be outside. Asking questions, chasing adventures—that was the life he wanted.

Growing up in Rhode Island and Connecticut, he set off on long rambles through forests and hills. One winter day, when he was just seven, Clarence raced home, thrilled by a strange sight. He dragged his mother, Florence, a mile down a snowy lane. He stopped at a stone wall and pointed. In one of the stones was the fossil of a fern.

The boy turned to his mother, demanding an explanation.

She didn't have one. Luckily for Clarence, she was the kind of mom to admit it, and to say, "Let's look it up." Together they pored through stacks of books on geology and natural history. From that point on, Florence King would recall, their home became "a veritable museum, where all kinds of specimens were studied with enthusiasm."

A year after earning a science degree from Yale, King set out on horseback for California. It was a journey that changed his life. As King crossed the West, he was endlessly amazed by soaring mountains and odd rock formations, sheer cliffs and winding canyons. Everyone saw these sights, but King's view was a bit different. Where others saw natural wonders, he saw stories. Epic stories with clashing characters such as volcanoes, glaciers, rivers, and wind. He could condense millions of years in his mind, watching nature's forces sculpt the awesome landscapes of the West.

These are the stories he wanted to tell. This, King decided, would be his life's work.

In 1867, still just twenty-five years old, Clarence King persuaded Congress to fund what became known as the Fortieth Parallel Survey. King's task was to study and map a massive stretch of land forty degrees north of the equator, from the Sierra Nevada in California all the way to Colorado's Rocky Mountains.

Nothing like this had ever been attempted. Along with the job came a cool title: Geologist in Charge.

King put together a team of scientific explorers, recruiting students as young as sixteen. Over the next five years, the group drew detailed maps, measured mountains, and took hundreds of photographs. They loaded mules with samples of plants, animals, and minerals. King and his crew traveled up to forty miles a day through burning heat and raging storms. Nearly everyone suffered sunstroke and battled malaria. They worked their way over mountains so high that they were covered with deep snow all summer. Travel by day was impossible on these slopes, as pack animals sank into the snow. They had to wait till after midnight, when plunging temperatures caused a layer of icy crust to form, before continuing their journey.

Now, in the summer of 1872, King's team was in the sixth and final year of their survey. King trekked across the Ruby Range of Nevada, while a second crew, led by Samuel Emmons and A. D. Wilson, finished up work in Utah and Wyoming. The geologists were far from newspapers or telegraph lines, but they'd pick up bits of news when they crossed paths with travelers or miners. The big story that summer was the discovery of a fantastically rich diamond mine somewhere in the West.

The whole thing sounded like a far-fetched fantasy. A bunch of humbug, King's men figured—until they heard that the mining engineer Henry Janin had inspected the field. Could that be true? The scientists knew Janin, "a man of undoubted integrity," Emmons said.

Anyway, the story didn't really impact them, King's team

assumed. According to most rumors, the mine was somewhere in the Southwest. Probably Arizona, far from the land of King's survey. It's not as if they'd missed a fabulous diamond mine on land they'd spent six years studying—now that would be embarrassing!

Clarence King updated his bosses in Washington that his crew was looking forward to finishing their job. "The summer has been one uninterrupted success," King wrote, "and the Expedition is practically done."

The survey was nearly done, sure.

But Clarence King's role in the story of the Great Diamond Hoax had just begun.

18

COMPETING CLAIMS

Lloyd MacIntyre was working on a farm near Elizabethtown, Kentucky, when he heard of an interesting opportunity. A rich guy named Philip Arnold was hiring a crew to work at some sort of mine out West. Arnold was offering $2.50 a day, a good wage at the time. The job included food, supplies—even promised a bit of travel and adventure.

MacIntyre was one of twenty young Black men from around Elizabethtown to sign on. With Arnold in the lead, the group headed west by rail. At a stop in Omaha, Nebraska, Arnold's crew got off the train and paraded through the city.

"Considerable curiosity was manifested by those who saw them march up town, with their arms and equipments," noted the *Omaha Daily Bee*.

A hunting expedition, Arnold told the reporter. The men camped behind a hotel, then hiked back to the train. When they reached Laramie, Wyoming, Arnold bought horses and plenty of food and ammunition. He and the other men from Kentucky marched and exercised near town—drawing lots of attention, as they had all the way west.

Like so much of Arnold's behavior that summer, this made no sense. Not at first glance, anyway.

Everyone wanted to know the location of the diamond field. And Arnold was known to have worked with the San Francisco diamond company. It was easy to guess that Arnold had come to Wyoming, with a crew of workers, to lead some sort of mission to the mine. Arnold was watched everywhere he went. If he left town, he'd certainly be followed. So why would he *try* to draw attention? How was he supposed to lead a survey team back to the diamond mine?

Here's one plausible explanation: Arnold never intended to return to the mine. What good could come of that? His goal was actually to make it *harder* for a survey team to get out there. This would lengthen the life of his game. Prolong the fun.

In San Francisco, the newspapers would not leave George Roberts alone. The diamond company had removed its display of gems—the constant crowds had made office work impossible. But reporters hung around, pestering Roberts for updates.

One eager reporter asked if Janin was already at the mine.

"Yes, he is," Roberts said, confirming reports that Henry Janin was already at the diamond field. "He expects to bring out, all the time he is down there, a million dollars a month."

Roberts and Harpending could only hope this was true. Janin had set out to meet Philip Arnold. The plan was for them to head to the mine together.

Instead, Janin and Arnold got stuck in Laramie together.

Janin's survey had to be done in absolute secret. The company needed to gain legal control of the field *before* its location became known, or the land would be overrun with miners. But of course the famous engineer was spotted the moment he arrived in town. He was watched like a thief, followed night and day. Miners tried to buy him drinks in saloons, hoping to pry loose clues to the country's favorite mystery.

Janin was annoyed and stressed even before reading George Roberts's quote in the newspaper. *A million dollars a month*? Janin had never said that! Those sorts of exaggerations would make the company look dishonest.

Also, why had Roberts said Janin was already at the mine? That was obviously false. People saw him in Laramie every day.

The engineer fired off coded telegrams to San Francisco, increasingly anxious in tone. He simply did not dare to leave town.

"There is a great deal of misery in store for those who go hunting for the North American diamond fields without more definite knowledge of its locality."

Sound advice from the *Sacramento Daily Union* that August.

Sound advice that had no chance of being heeded.

While Arnold drilled with his men, and Janin hid in his hotel room, hopeful miners set out on expeditions to find the diamond field. Newspapers all over the West encouraged the rush. Many declared that their towns just happened to be the best place to buy gear for the search.

"It is becoming well known that Santa Fe is the most convenient road to the mines," announced a New Mexico paper.

The *Daily Denver Times* urged diamond hunters to try their

luck in Colorado. "The Times will offer a splendid premium to the first one found in Colorado."

Arizona drew diamond prospectors, along with Utah and Wyoming—all within the "1,000 miles to the east of Ralston's office" clue offered by a diamond company official. Of course, none of these destinations were anywhere near the diamond mine.

The fake diamond mine, that is.

"This is all old to me," an Arizona saloonkeeper informed San Francisco's *Daily Alta California*. "I have known of the existence of diamonds in New Mexico for years."

Here is another classic element of successful scams—they take on a life of their own. People not only believe the fable; they start adding their own creative layers.

George W. Fox, a miner from Nevada, told newspapers he knew *exactly* where the diamond field was. How? Well, the summer before he'd secretly tracked Phil Arnold out there.

In Arizona.

Another miner—named Tom Miner!—was greatly annoyed by all this sharing of information. Described by reporters as small and forceful, Miner swore he'd found the diamond mine before Slack and Arnold.

In Arizona.

Tom Miner was now in Frisco, working on the process of claiming the land. And the San Francisco and New York Mining and Commercial Company had better watch out! "I am going back," Miner told a *Chronicle* reporter, "and if they have taken our ground, I am going to have it."

"Miner is a bilk," George Roberts fired back. "He never discovered our diamond-fields at all, and don't know where they are."

Undaunted by his rival's fancy offices and high-priced lawyers, Tom Miner predicted victory. He also offered Roberts a word of warning: "He had better not call me names."

Philip Arnold followed the swirling controversy from Laramie. For the past year, he'd ducked interviews, avoided the press.

Now, Arnold announced, he had something he wanted to say.

19

TWO ARNOLDS

"I am the original discoverer of the Diamond District." So declared a man named Arnold.

Mr. T. Edward Arnold, to be precise.

T. Edward was a lean man of about forty. Dark hair, blue-gray eyes, bristly mustache. Yes, this was Philip Arnold. Why was he suddenly calling himself T. Edward? Hard to say. Did he really think this would disguise his true identity? More likely, he was just having fun.

People do weird things. Maybe you've noticed.

Anyway, he agreed to sit down for an interview with Laramie's *Daily Independent*. Ever since coming to town, he'd been harassed by hopeful miners. Some tried to bribe him for information. Others tried threats of violence. Now, T. Edward said, he wanted to set the record straight.

Was it true, the writer asked, that Arnold was in town on a mission for this new San Francisco diamond company every-one was talking about?

"You have got us down to a hole," Arnold said. "I came here for the purpose of fitting out an expedition as you state, supposing it could be done without our intentions or destination being discovered."

Arnold told of finding his diamond field three years before. "So plenty were the gems to be found that I picked up a quart or more in a few minutes." He had returned several times, bringing along his mining partner—a fellow called "Captain Steek."

"This is one that I brought out with me on my last trip," Arnold said, holding out a diamond of about seven carats, a good half inch across.

"A beautiful brilliant," remarked the reporter.

Arnold's goal now was to get back to the site. This was going to be tough, given how closely he was being watched.

What about George W. Fox and Tom Miner? The men saying they'd found the site first?

"The San Francisco papers have been working in the dark, publishing all sorts of nonsense," Arnold said. He scoffed at the mention of Fox and Miner. "I know them both well; they are frauds."

In a follow-up interview in Laramie, the man calling himself T. Edward Arnold dropped another bombshell.

"There are so many people going into that country, that it cannot be kept a secret any longer," he said. "The diamond fields prevail over quite a range of country in New Mexico, on the border of Arizona."

Finally, the secret was out!

In San Francisco, reporters raced to George Roberts's office for a reaction.

"I was much surprised at seeing the statement," Roberts said.

One writer described Roberts as reserved, worried, not his usual outgoing self. You get the sense he was desperately struggling to keep calm as events around him spun out of control.

Why was Phil Arnold suddenly talking to the press? Why on earth was he calling himself T. Edward Arnold?

And . . . Captain *Steek*?

Was that supposed to be a cleverly disguised version of Slack?

Best not to deny Arnold's strange stories, Roberts reckoned. Actually, the lie about the mine being in New Mexico might even prove helpful. "I cannot enlighten you at present in regard to its truth," he said of Arnold's New Mexico revelation. Let readers draw their own—hopefully incorrect—conclusions.

Diamond fever soared higher and higher, turning into a nationwide frenzy. Optimistic investors launched at least twenty-five new diamond companies, preparing to issue the modern equivalent of many billions of dollars' worth of stock.

Tom Miner still claimed he'd found the mine first. He formed the Original Diamond Discovery and Mining Company and raised a small fortune by selling thousands of shares of stock. He placed an ad in San Francisco papers, looking to hire tough guys to join an expedition to his site—and to drive Roberts and Harpending's company off the land.

Competing companies formed in Arizona, Nevada, Utah, and Colorado. "Denver was, indeed, ablaze with excitement," the city's *Tribune* recalled later. "Everybody was either president, vice-president or prospector of a diamond company."

There'd soon be five thousand men searching the West for diamonds, newspapers predicted. "On my way up to Santa Fe," one old-time miner reported, "I saw not less than one hundred and fifty parties wending their way in search of the gems."

The race was on, while Roberts and Harpending sat still in San Francisco.

Watching the bonanza of a lifetime slip from their grasp.

Harpending told Arnold to pay off the men from Kentucky and send them home. It was obvious Arnold's crew was never going to make it to the mine without being followed.

Harpending and Roberts hadn't heard from Henry Janin in a while and held out hope that the engineer had made it out to the diamond field without Arnold. Then more bad news arrived, in the form of an alarming report in the Sacramento *Daily Bee*: "It is rumored on the street today that Janin, agent of the Diamond Company, has been murdered on his way here with several million dollars' worth of diamonds."

Murdered! Had Janin been ambushed on the road? Forced to reveal the mine's location?

Roberts and Harpending reached new levels of panic before Janin stumbled into Frisco—very much alive, but badly rattled and done with trying to return to the diamond field. Sick of being followed and questioned, Janin even wanted to sell his stock. The company partners quietly bought the engineer's shares for $40 each, far below what they'd have fetched on the open market.

This solved nothing. Roberts and Harpending had sunk hundreds of thousands of dollars into this venture. They were on the brink of losing it all because the company still didn't have legal control of the diamond field. They were absolutely desperate to get a survey team out to their field before someone else found it. But how? Any expedition would be watched and followed.

That was the problem. But . . . was it also the solution?

Asbury Harpending had a devious thought. If it was impossible to launch a real expedition, why not send out a fake one?

20

TWO EXPEDITIONS

Twenty men crowded into Asbury Harpending's office, a mix of grizzled miners, young adventurers, and tenderfoot clerks in search of excitement.

Harpending explained the deal. This was a four-month commitment. The group would travel where he directed them. They'd search for gold, silver, and, yes, precious stones. Harpending would buy all supplies, pay all expenses. The men would get a share of any discoveries. To lead the expedition, Harpending introduced Mike Gray, a man he'd worked with and trusted. A tough westerner in his mid-forties, Gray had served in the Texas Rangers as a teen and later as sheriff of Yuba County, California.

Everyone signed on. They agreed to meet at the Oakland ferry station early the next morning.

"Where are you going?" people asked the men that night.

"When do you start?"

It was impossible to hide a new expedition, especially one originating in Asbury Harpending's office. Harpending was the diamond big shot. Everyone knew what he was up to.

Or thought they did.

"Each man is sworn to secrecy," noted a California newspaper. "No swallowing of big diamonds or similar tricks will be allowed."

As the team traveled east from Oakland, Mike Gray told the men they'd be at the diamond field in fifteen days. "Keep quiet," Gray warned, "and have as little to say as possible."

All agreed. They expected to be rich very soon.

A few days later, Gray's group was spotted in Denver—"fierce looking fellows," noted the *Daily Rocky Mountain News.* Curious citizens followed the strangers around, hoping to overhear hints of their travel plans. Mike Gray was vague about their destination. He insisted his team was in search of gold and silver, not diamonds.

No one bought it.

"Let them go by what route they may," another newspaper commented, "they are certain of being followed."

Mike Gray knew he'd be followed. Actually, this was his job. Harpending's private instructions to Gray were clear: Walk southwest out of Colorado and get yourself lost for a few months.

The only other person in on the secret was Gray's assistant, a man named Jones.

With all eyes on Gray's group, Harpending put together a second expedition in San Francisco. This is a classic magician's move. Direct your audience's attention one way, then perform your sleight of hand unseen. The trick, in this case, was getting this second expedition—a real surveying team—out of town without being noticed.

George Roberts agreed to lead the outing. It was fitting. Hadn't the country's raging diamond fever begun in his office less than two years before?

"Everything was done with rigid and complete secrecy," remembered Dr. Charles Cleveland, who was recruited for the team. Alfred Rubery, who'd been to the mine earlier that year, agreed to guide the group. He was always eager for adventure and felt pretty sure he remembered the way to the diamond field.

Roberts approached trusted friends to round out the crew.

"Gillette, you are looking thin," Roberts said to his pal Martin F. Gillette on the street in San Francisco. "You need recreation, fresh country air and great expectations. What do you say—will you take a tramp with me?"

Gillette was intrigued. "George, I'll follow. Lead on."

Traveling by ones and twos, Roberts and his team slipped out of town in late August. Harpending—usually the optimist—fought off a wave of doubt.

"I hope you will get there," he told Dr. Cleveland, "but I am afraid you won't. If you get there, Doctor, you will find one of the biggest things in the world."

Now back to the fake expedition.

Riding horses and leading pack mules, Mike Gray guided twenty men out of Pueblo, the end of the railroad line in southeastern Colorado. A violent thunderstorm lashed the group as they set up tents south of town. Some of the men began to think this trip might not be so pleasant.

Several groups of travelers camped a short distance behind them.

"Shall we allow those men to follow us?" Gray's men protested. "We can not permit them to track us in that way."

For some reason, Gray and his assistant Jones did not seem concerned.

A week of hard travel later, the party was somewhere in New Mexico. Jones stopped often to check his maps. He'd been to the diamond field, or so he claimed. The men turned to him often for updates.

"When will our journey end?" was a common question.

"Pretty soon," he'd say.

And: "Just across the next range of mountains."

And: "If I don't prove what I say, you can do what you choose with me."

A risky promise to make to a bunch of guys who'd find out, at some point, they were nothing more than props in a magic trick.

"We crossed and recrossed mountains and valleys," one of the men later recalled. They ran low on food and water. The men grumbled bitterly as Gray put everyone on half rations. The followers gradually dropped off. One last group stayed on Gray's tail for five hundred miles before giving up.

Gray's party was finally alone, somewhere in New Mexico, riding exhausted animals farther and farther from the diamond field.

Far to the north, Roberts and his team gathered just outside the town of Green River, Wyoming.

"We are going to the diamond fields," Alfred Rubery told his group. "I may have some difficulty in recognizing the spot."

Not exactly history's greatest pep talk.

The ten-man team rode south for several days, trudging through rugged high desert. Annoyingly, another party tracked them, camping each night about a mile and a half back. Rubery changed course.

"We went a very roundabout way," he'd later say, "partly because we were dodging the party who were following us."

He admitted to another reason as well: "Partly because we did not know our way."

The group tracking them ran out of food and gave up. Rubery led on another week, up and down steep slopes, along the rims of deep canyons. They were nearly out of water, and there was not a drop in sight.

"It's very strange," an irritated Dr. Cleveland commented, "that a man should have been in the country and not be able to find it again."

Rubery got defensive. Sure, he'd been to the mine, but Slack and Arnold had led the group on a winding route—even the cousins had seemed lost at the time. Besides, that was spring, and there was snow on the mountains, which made the landscape look different. Anyway, he was from England. How was he supposed to tell one scrubby hill from another?

Dr. Cleveland was unmoved. He called the trip "an ordeal of the most wearing, arduous, uncertain, violent, exasperating, perilous nature that it was possible to conceive."

The weary travelers pestered Rubery with endless complaints and questions.

"When will we reach the diamond fields?"

"Are we on the right track now?" This was the nineteenth-century version of a kid in the back seat of a car asking, "Are we there yet?"

They were not there yet.

PART 5

BRILLIANT CITY

Philip Arnold next showed up in Denver, Colorado.
SLOAN HOUSE
SALOON & SLEEPING PLACE
SALOON & SLEEPING PLACE
SUNDRI

Arnold hinted, but refused to confirm . . .

. . . that his gems were found in Arizona or New Mexico.

In an interview with the *Rocky Mountain News*, he bizarrely claimed that the Arnold who'd recently been interviewed in Laramie, Wyoming—that wasn't him.
Never been to Laramie. Someone 'personated me.

Arnold left for Laramie, supposedly to find and expose the "fake" Arnold.
"It seems to us not at all probable that a collision of Arnolds will ensue..."

Mike Gray's decoy party was hopelessly lost somewhere in the Southwest—exactly as planned.

We had ceased to think of diamonds or gold. Water was what we cried for.

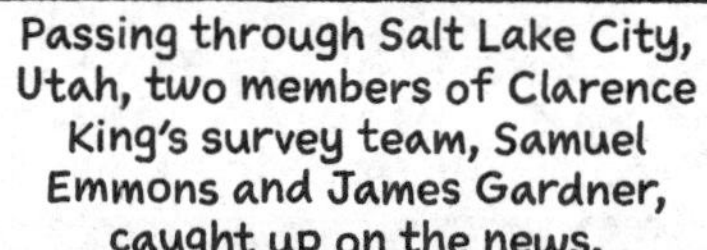
Passing through Salt Lake City, Utah, two members of Clarence King's survey team, Samuel Emmons and James Gardner, caught up on the news.

Newspaper reports confirmed that Henry Janin had inspected the diamond mine and declared it genuine.
I'd scarcely give the story a passing thought—if the name Janin weren't connected with it.

Was it possible they'd missed a diamond bonanza on land they'd spent six years studying?

They wanted to go check the mine for themselves—but how could they possibly find it?

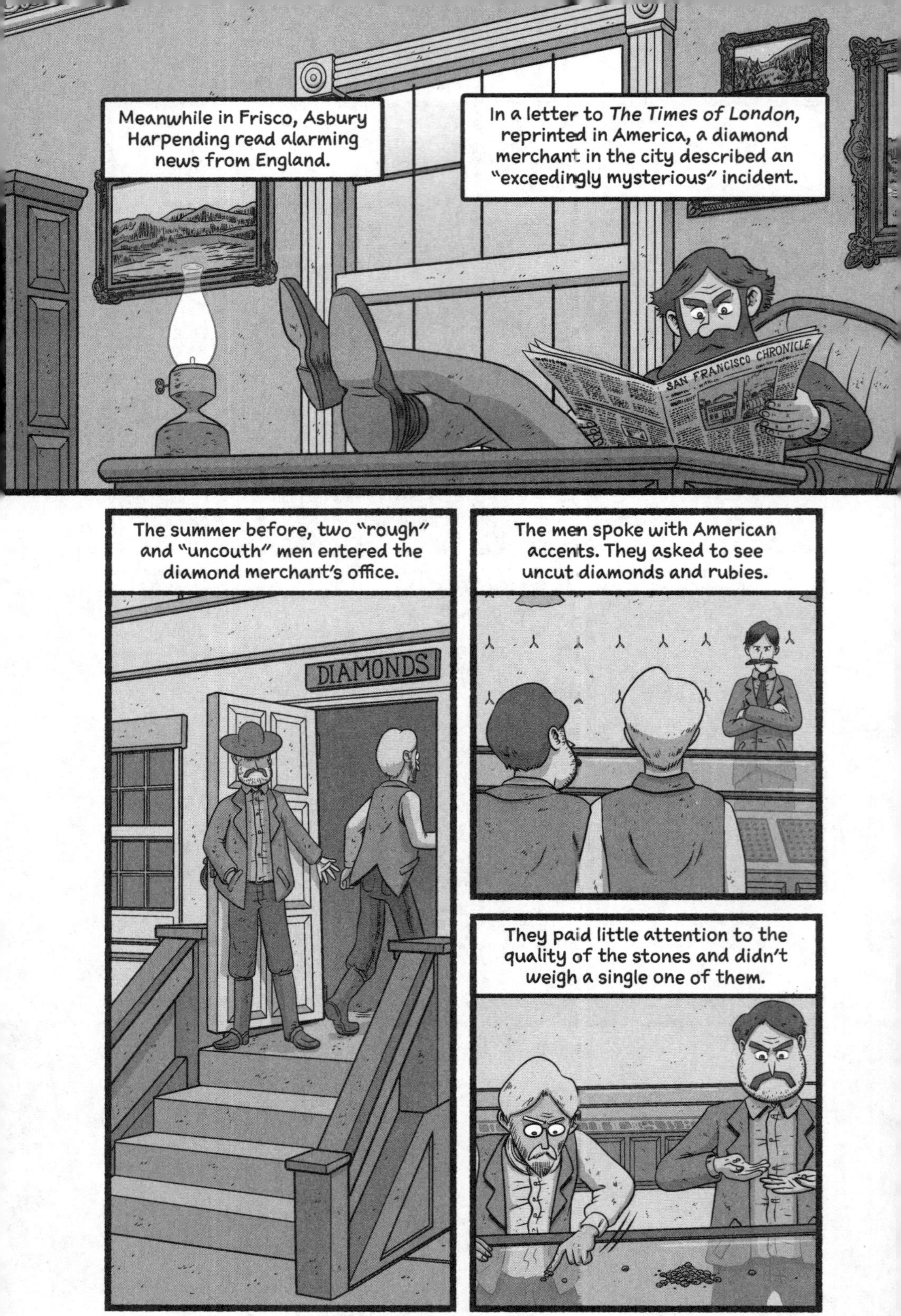

Meanwhile in Frisco, Asbury Harpending read alarming news from England.

In a letter to *The Times of London*, reprinted in America, a diamond merchant in the city described an "exceedingly mysterious" incident.

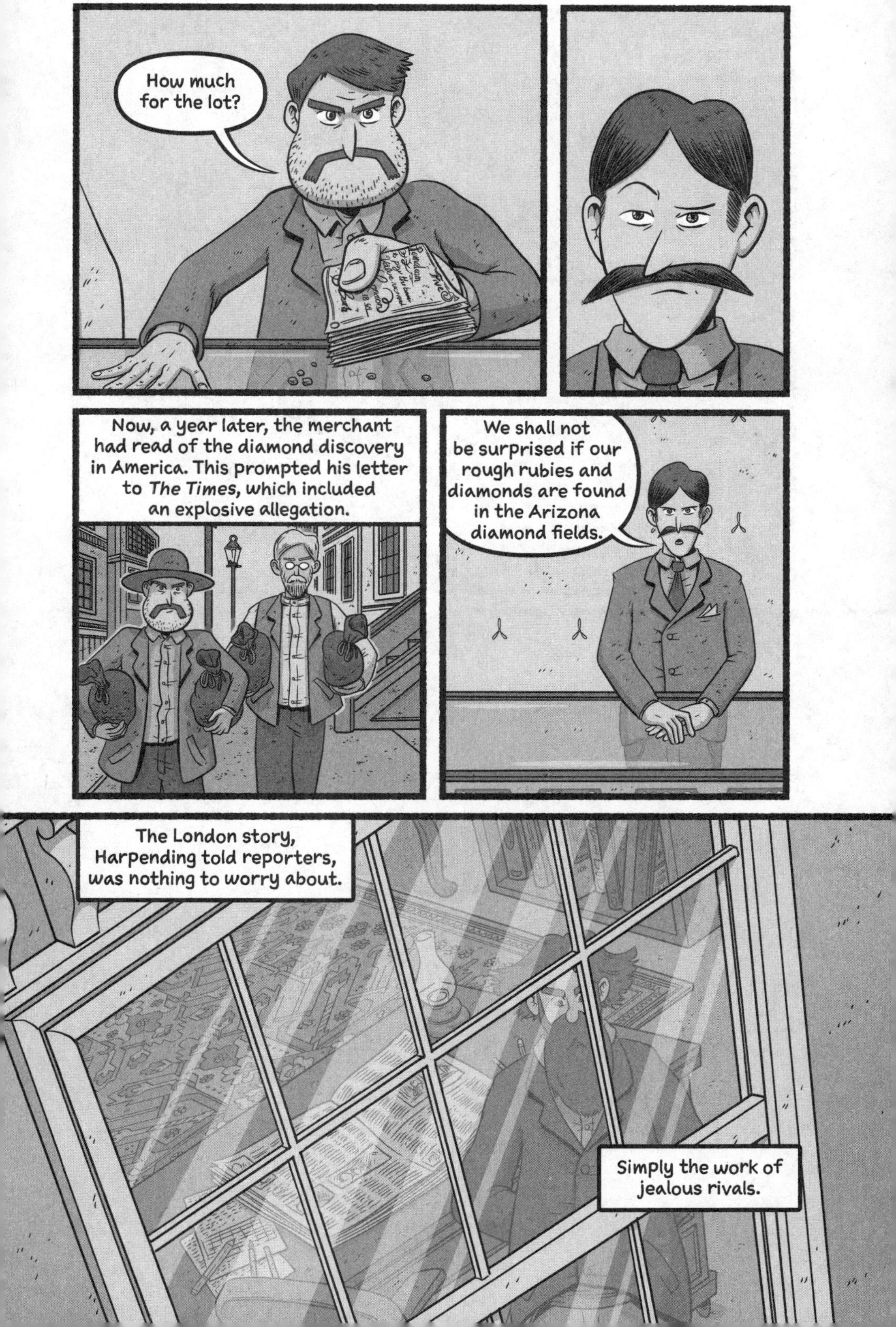

Now, a year later, the merchant had read of the diamond discovery in America. This prompted his letter to *The Times*, which included an explosive allegation.

The London story, Harpending told reporters, was nothing to worry about.

Simply the work of jealous rivals.

It was the wrong mountain.

21

GLITTER AND FLASH

A man stepped into a jewelry store on Kearny Street in San Francisco. Burned by the sun, dusty from travel, he called the owner to a quiet corner of the shop. He lifted a package from his pocket, set it on the counter, and unwrapped the cloth covering. Inside was a small pile of stones, glittering and flashing in sunlight angling in from the window.

"These are about two or three ounces of Arizona diamonds in the rough," the man told the jeweler. He'd heard the diamond stories. Caught the fever. He'd gone searching in the Southwest and had bought this pile from a fellow who'd actually been to the mine.

"I am positive that the whole lot are diamonds," the man said.

He wanted them tested, just to be sure he'd made a good bargain. This sort of thing was becoming common. People kept turning up in cities with gems they'd found—or bought at an amazing bargain. They were rich!

Maybe.

The jeweler tested the hardness of the stones by trying to scratch other minerals with them. He peered into them with his magnifying loupe . . .

And told his visitor he'd been hoaxed. He'd bought a pile of pretty quartz crystals.

"The information that his pebbles were not jewels so shocked the stranger that he staggered pale and agitated to a chair," reported the *San Francisco Chronicle.* "Restoratives had to be applied to prevent his fainting."

A few blocks away, at the headquarters of the San Francisco and New York Mining and Commercial Company, Asbury Harpending was also fainting—or trying not to. Company officials were bombarded with questions about the London diamond merchant who said he'd sold sacks of rough diamonds to two Americans. Could they have been Slack and Arnold?

"This news did not disturb me," company president William Lent told reporters. "I thought it was a trick of the trade."

This was their agreed-upon strategy. Appear calm. Deny any possibility that their diamonds were purchased in London. And suggest an alternative explanation for the London story: European jewelers were worried that the center of the world's gem industry was about to move to America. So they were spreading this bogus story out of fear and jealousy. Trick of the trade.

Privately, Harpending, Lent, and friends were seriously concerned—and not only about the London diamond merchant. It had been nearly a month, and there was *still* no word from Roberts and Rubery.

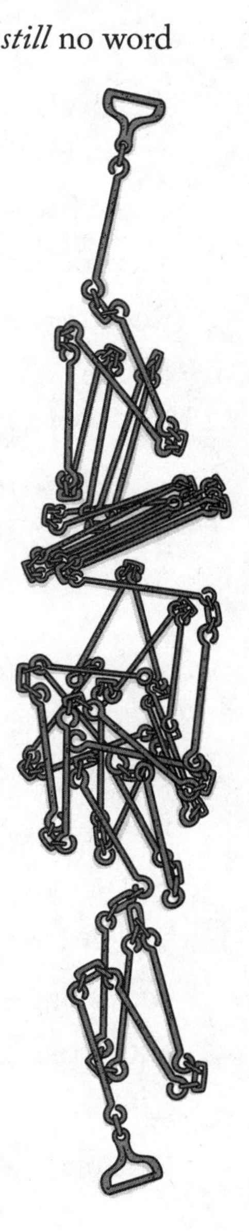

"This is the place," declared Alfred Rubery, "and that is our spring, and down there is the diamond field."

About time.

Four weeks after leaving Green River, Rubery had finally found the field. The men cheered and dove to the ground, chopping holes in the gravel with long knives. Before sunset, they'd all found diamonds and rubies.

But their job, sadly, was not to gather riches. The crew spent a week lugging surveying chains across the mesa and up and down the surrounding slopes. Each chain was a specific length, allowing them to accurately measure the land the company wanted to claim. They even mapped out the site of a future town: Brilliant City.

The men took turns standing guard all night,

shivering in the autumn wind, watching stars arc across the massive black sky. George Roberts showed off the outdoor cooking skills he'd learned as a miner twenty years before. "Roberts turned out the first loaf of bread baked on the ground," Martin Gillette remembered, "and it was bully."

Mission accomplished, the team trekked back to the railroad. This time they went the right way. It took only two days.

In San Francisco, Harpending was thrilled to get a telegram from Roberts. The survey crew was on its way back! But Roberts's telegram was so short and secretive, Harpending couldn't tell how the trip had gone. William Lent jumped on a train and headed east to meet the group in Sacramento.

A newspaper reporter shadowed Lent, determined to get the story.

At the same time, two members of Clarence King's Fortieth Parallel Survey boarded a westbound train in Battle Mountain, Nevada.

Samuel Emmons and James Gardner were done for the season, and nearly finished with six exhausting years of work. Snow was falling already, small streams icing overnight. Time to get out of the mountains, back to a warm hotel. The plan was for King's whole team to meet up in San Francisco, then travel to Washington, D.C., to begin writing their final reports.

Emmons and Gardner had been hearing diamond stories all year. The fact that Henry Janin was involved impressed them. They knew Janin personally and respected his work. There must really be diamonds out there, which sparked their scientific curiosity. What did a diamond mine look like? No one had ever seen one in North America. Until now, apparently. But the mine was rumored to be in far-off New Mexico or Arizona. And they had work to do in Frisco.

The train rolled across Nevada and into California, chugging high into the Sierra Nevada as the sun rose over snowy peaks. The geologists were eating breakfast when a group of passengers, about ten men, strolled into the dining car. Rough clothes and muddy boots, scruffy beards and windblown hair. Not your typical tourists.

This was George Roberts's surveying party. A chance encounter that would change everything.

Emmons didn't know the men. He guessed they were miners. Diamond hunters? Could be. They seemed happy. Satisfied, as if they'd had a successful trip. It was a bit worrying, actually. Suppose they *were* diamond miners. They were awfully far from the Southwest. Could the mine be a lot farther north than anyone realized?

Then came the shocker.

When the train stopped at Alta, California, Henry Janin climbed aboard. The famous mining engineer! What was he doing here? Janin glanced around and spotted the group of miners. He huddled with them, talking in low tones. Smiling, shaking hands, clapping backs.

That confirmed it. The miners were diamond company men from Frisco. Had to be.

For Clarence King's geologists, this was the worst possible news. The mine must be somewhere fairly near the transcontinental railroad, which ran just north of the Fortieth Parallel. *Could the diamonds be on the very land they'd just finished studying?*

That would be a disaster for King's team. They'd spent six years exploring and mapping this section of land, studying its geology and natural resources. If they somehow missed a diamond mine, people would assume they'd done a pretty poor job. Clarence King would be a national laughingstock. Imagine the humiliating headlines . . .

"GEOLOGIST IN CHARGE" DOESN'T NOTICE WORLD'S BIGGEST DIAMOND MINE

Emmons and Gardner needed to act. Six years of work depended on it. The reputation of their beloved boss was at stake. One way or another, they *had* to figure out exactly where those diamond hunters had been.

22

THE DIAMONDIFEROUS LOCALITY

When Henry Janin was done talking with the diamond company men, he noticed Emmons and Gardner and stepped over to chat. Yes, Janin confirmed, those dusty fellows had just been out to the famous diamond field. The men were there to survey the land, Janin explained, not to search for diamonds—though they'd managed to dig up a few brilliants. Janin held out his hand, displaying a small sample.

"Very clear fine stones," recalled Emmons, "varying in size from that of a grain of wheat to a small pea."

Where exactly, Emmons asked, had these precious stones been found?

Janin understood the geologists' curiosity. And he said he'd happily tell them "the diamondiferous locality," as he called it—only he was still employed by the diamond company and had been sworn to secrecy. In any case, Janin said, the company had to wait until spring to begin mining. The diamond field was at a high elevation and would be difficult to reach in winter.

This was a clue. Not nearly enough information to find the place, but it was a start.

Hoping to learn more, Emmons and Gardner struck up conversations with men from the surveying trip. The geologists acted only mildly interested in the diamond mine. Just passing the time, really. It worked. One of the surveyors asked Gardner a bunch of questions about the exact boundary lines between Colorado, Wyoming, and Utah. Another clue.

Other miners mentioned that there was good timber near the diamond field. And that streams froze overnight. And that, returning from the mine, the crew had boarded the railroad in western Wyoming. All valuable leads.

Still, finding the exact spot would require an all-time great bit of detective work.

The reporter who followed William Lent from San Francisco had a long, hot wait at the Sacramento train station. He stood out of sight, watching Lent. The diamond company president seemed anxious, impatient.

Finally, the westbound train pulled in. Passengers poured onto the platform.

A large man stepped out. Filthy clothes, unshaven for a

month or more, a long knife in his belt. He let loose an explosive sneeze, blasting sand from each nostril.

Must be a miner, thought the reporter. Sure enough, William Lent walked right up to the sneezer. They shook hands.

"Where is Roberts?" Lent asked.

The large guy pointed toward a sleeping car. Lent leapt up a set of steps onto the train.

Another man stepped off, smaller than the sneezer but just as dirty, "with a shocking bad hat," noted the reporter. This was Alfred Rubery. The larger man was Martin Gillette.

Rubery said, "Gillette, let us get a nobbler; I'm very dry."

While the two miners went for a drink, the reporter followed Lent onto the train. He found Lent sitting with George Roberts. Lent looked twenty years younger than he had just five minutes before.

The reporter marched up, asking for the latest news from the diamond field.

"Nothing whatever, sir," Lent said. He seemed mighty pleased about nothing.

"Nothing whatever?"

"Nothing. Party got lost," Lent said, "and came back."

George Roberts was a bit less reserved. The field was real, he said, and very rich indeed.

"When do you intend to return and commence vigorous operations?" asked the reporter.

"Not before spring," Roberts said. "The place is too cold for winter operations, and besides, we have a great many arrangements to make." As for any more details, that would have to wait. The company needed to gain full legal control of the land and get a force out there to guard the site. Only then would its location be made public.

The secret was safe for months to come. Or so Roberts believed.

George Roberts returned to San Francisco a conquering hero. His mission had taken a bit longer than expected, but it was a total success. Nothing stood in the way of the company taking full legal control of the mine. "Every holder of the company's stock figured on being a millionaire at least by the early spring," recalled Asbury Harpending.

Reporters continued pumping Roberts and Harpending for leads about the mine's location. No luck. One thing seemed clear: The diamond company men were more confident than ever about the richness of their field. "If they have been deceived," the *Evening Bulletin* quoted Roberts as saying, "they are the worst deceived and cheated men who ever lived."

The London diamond merchant's story was totally forgotten.

23

CARBONIFEROUS FOSSILS

This wasn't like searching for a needle in a haystack. It was like searching for a needle in a giant field of hay.

Clarence King's team was upset by the possibility that the diamond field was on land they had surveyed. The scientists needed to figure out the location of the mine, but it seemed an impossible challenge. The search area was simply too big.

Besides, hadn't thousands of people been out looking all year, with no success?

Or was that a clue in itself? Everyone must be looking in the wrong place.

Clarence King was still in the Sierras studying glaciers and would be out of touch for at least another week. In the meantime, the Fortieth Parallel team attacked the mystery with a clever mix of scientific logic and hands-on detective work. Working individually, they managed to casually bump into men who'd been out to the mine with Henry Janin or George Roberts. They weren't asking for priceless secrets about the mine's location—heaven forbid! But, as scientists, they were curious about the features of the land. Distinctive rock formations, types of vegetation, "and various other things," recalled A. D. Wilson, "that would mean nothing to an ordinary individual, but to us, with our knowledge of the country, would mean much."

Each evening, the team met at the Montgomery Block building. Walking through a lobby with potted palm trees and clouds of cigar smoke, the men gathered in Clarence King's office upstairs. They compared notes. Cross-checked findings. Focused in on a handful of essential clues and the likely meaning of each.

"The information thus gathered was rather meagre," Samuel Emmons later said, "and might seem to some of a very trifling petty character, but with our intimate knowledge of the geology and topography of the region it was sufficient to determine for us the precise locality, within a radius of perhaps fifteen miles."

Clarence King returned to San Francisco on the night of October 19. He'd been hearing diamond rumors too and had gathered a few clues of his own.

"Where do you think the diamond fields are?" Emmons asked.

"They are not in Arizona," King said. "I am convinced of that."

CLUE: When Henry Janin visited the mine in June, the whole team left the railroad somewhere in Wyoming. They traveled on horses and mules. The group was back on the train three weeks later.
SIGNIFICANCE: They could not have gone to Arizona or New Mexico and back in that amount of time. The diamond mine was not in the Southwest.
Henry Janin..
CLUE: Janin's crew camped on a stone mesa at the foot of a mountain covered with pine trees. There was snow on the peak of the mountain. Nights were cold.
SIGNIFICANCE: The field was at a high elevation. The wooded mountain was higher still, but not massive. The timberline in the West is around 11,000 feet—trees don't grow above this elevation.
CARMINE
11,000'
CLUE: Members of Roberts's survey group also mentioned a wooded mountain. They camped on the north side of the mountain. There were no taller peaks in sight.
SIGNIFICANCE: The diamond field must be just north of the mountain. It was not in the Colorado Rockies, where peaks over 12,000 feet were common. The description of the land sounded more like the high desert of Wyoming.
ROCKIES
DESERT
29
30
28
31
27
25
26
CLUE: A member of Roberts's team asked questions about the exact boundaries of Colorado, Wyoming, and Utah.
SIGNIFICANCE: He must not have known for certain which territory the mine was in—this would be hard to determine in a very remote area. The mine must be close to the spot where these three territories met, or why ask this specific question?
WY
?
UT
CO

"Well," Emmons said, "what would you consider the most probable location from a geological point of view?"

Looking at all the evidence, King agreed with his team. The logical conclusion was alarming. "I was certain there was only one place in that country which answered the description," King later recalled. "That place lay within the limits of the Fortieth Parallel Survey."

All were in agreement—they had to search for the diamond field and study it themselves. This wasn't about finding gems; it was about uncovering the truth.

And they had to leave *now*.

It was too late in the year to travel there safely, but that didn't matter. "It would be a blight on any geological survey not to have known of its existence," King said, "and I had to do it as a matter of self-defense."

The team gathered supplies, including a diamond-tipped blade for testing the hardness of minerals. To hide the true purpose of their journey, they spread word that they had one last bit of fieldwork to do for their survey. And they agreed never to use the word *diamonds* aloud—they'd only refer to "carboniferous fossils."

Leaving at different times to evade prying eyes, King's team traveled east by train in late October.

* * *

Most miners were heading the other way, back to towns for the winter. The search for diamonds would continue in the spring. Tom Miner's Original Diamond Discovery and Mining Company kept a small team at his mine to guard the "real" diamond field.

In Arizona.

Asbury Harpending and George Roberts shared a laugh about this. Poor Tom wasn't within five hundred miles of pay dirt!

Nearly two years after the cousins from Kentucky stumbled into Frisco with their rough gems, everything was in place. Harpending and Roberts had spent their lives searching for their own Sutter's Mill, the strike that launched the Gold Rush. They'd made some good finds, but this diamond mine—which they now legally controlled—was on a whole different scale. Finally, it was time to put millions of dollars' worth of stock on the market and watch it soar!

"If all the stories and theories in circulation are true," observed one Frisco paper, "San Francisco will within a few months contain more wealthy people than any other city in the world."

24

FULL BELIEVERS

Clarence King, Samuel Emmons, and A. D. Wilson met at Fort Bridger, an army fort just south of the railroad through Wyoming. They had left mules and camping gear at the fort at the end of the summer, thinking none of it would be needed anytime soon. Soldiers stationed at Bridger warned King not to travel into the wilderness with winter setting in. When they saw King's crew packing shovels, they figured the scientists expected to be buried in snow.

King's team set out from Fort Bridger on October 29, with a small camp staff who had no idea where they were headed or why. It was a miserable journey for both mule and man, 150 miles through blizzards. As temperatures plunged below zero, Emmons layered four flannel shirts beneath his coat and still shivered. When the animals crossed shallow streams, their hooves broke through thin ice, and rushing water splashed onto their legs and froze like casts. They trudged on, limbs clicking as the ice broke apart and fell to the frigid ground.

When a particularly vicious gust of wind whipped across the high desert, Wilson, Emmons, and King looked at one another—all thinking the same thing, Wilson figured. A line from Shakespeare came to mind: "What fools these mortals be!"

Was this a fools' quest? They had to at least wonder.

Were they even going the right way?

On the fifth day out of Bridger, the searchers rode into a deep gulch between stone mesas. A dry creek bed snaked through the valley, its source frozen solid at higher elevations.

To the south was a gently sloped peak, covered with pine trees, rising to maybe 10,000 feet.

As the camp crew put up tents and gathered firewood, King, Wilson, and Emmons set out to explore a bit more before sunset. They were close. They had to be. Or everything they'd based this journey on was wrong.

King saw it first. A slip of paper flapping in the wind, nailed to a scrawny tree.

Rushing over, he read the writing on the paper. A claim of rights to the water running through the gulch. Dated June 15, 1872.

Signed by Henry Janin.

Scrambling onto the mesa, the geologists found more claims nailed to posts stuck into the ground. All of this land was claimed by the San Francisco and New York Mining and Commercial Company. Incredibly, they'd found it!

Wilson would recall feeling just a moment of doubt. "It seemed strange that all of this supposed wealth should be left there with no one in possession."

But this *must* be the spot—a sandstone plateau covered with reddish dirt and loose pebbles. People had been here recently, that was clear. There were boot prints in the sand, holes dug here and there. The men fell to their knees to inspect the frigid earth. Wilson found a small grayish stone and passed it around. King tested its hardness.

It was a diamond.

And then a very strange thing happened. Or maybe a very normal thing. Three experienced scientists were transformed, as if by magic spell, into giddy children. Scurrying across the ground, they chopped up fistfuls of earth and sifted dirt through bare hands. Their fingers went numb with cold, and they could barely hold the small gems they found. Three more diamonds! A small mound of rubies!

Sitting around the fire that night, the geologists congratulated one another on finding the spot that thousands had failed to discover. For the moment, all thoughts of scientific surveys were set aside.

Diamond fever had struck again.

"That night we were full believers," Samuel Emmons later confessed, "and dreamed of the untold wealth that might be gathered."

PART 6

KING OF DIAMONDS

Early the next morning.
Putting aside dreams of riches, King's team began a scientific investigation of the diamond field.
A genuine diamond field would have gems of all sizes, including tiny crystals.
No trace of microscopic diamonds.

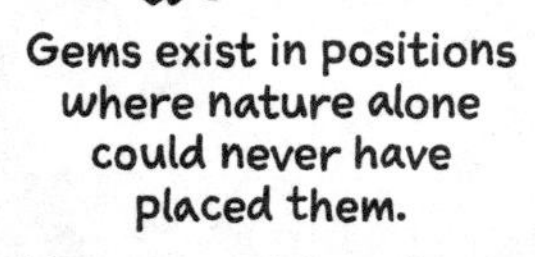

They do not exist where, had the occurrence been genuine, the inevitable laws of nature must have carried them.

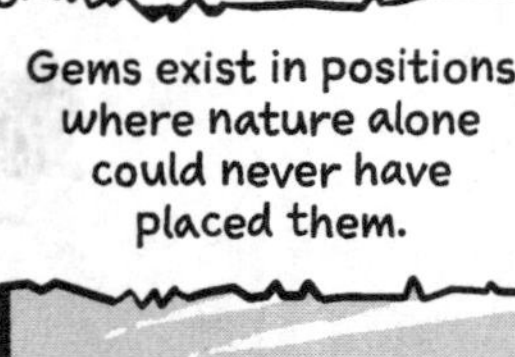

Over thousands of years, diamonds, which are heavier than sand, should have settled to the bedrock.

There were no gems deep beneath the surface. This was conclusive.
It's a fraud.

We've been followed!

Gentlemen.
Found any carats around here?

25

STARTLING FACTS

"Found any carats around here?"

Carats—a unit of weight for precious gems. The well-dressed gent strolling onto the field had come in search of diamonds.

Introducing himself as Mr. J. F. Berry, a jeweler from New York, he explained that he'd traveled west, determined to find the mine at any cost. He'd hired men to follow Henry Janin all summer, and others to watch railroad stops in Wyoming. He and his team spotted Clarence King's group and had been on their tail since they left Fort Bridger.

"We have been watching you from the top of yonder mountain with spyglasses, and bitter cold work it was," Berry said. "We knew that it must be diamonds and not fossils you were after, and have come down here to get some."

King did not deny that he'd come to study the diamond field. But the mine was a fraud, he told Berry. There were gems here, lots of them. But after careful scientific investigation, King and his team were now certain it was all just a clever hoax.

"You say it's a swindle?" Berry asked. "What a chance to sell short!"

If you think a stock price is going to fall, you can "sell short"—essentially, you can bet against the stock. Berry could make a fortune with what he'd just learned.

"No, that would not be an honorable thing to do," King said. "It is bad enough as it is."

The jeweler, without comment, walked off to rejoin his friends.

That evening, King huddled around a fire with Samuel Emmons and A. D. Wilson. Coyote howls drifted through camp on icy wind.

They could see J. F. Berry's campfire in the distance.

"That man will make mischief if he has the chance," King said.

Time was short. Unless it was exposed right away, the diamond fraud would do enormous damage to the economy of California and beyond. And aside from whoever had salted this mine—and the jeweler camping nearby—the three scientists were the only people who knew the truth.

King asked, "How can we reach the railroad in the quickest way from here?"

Wilson, a skilled mapmaker, told King that Black Buttes was the closest station. Forty miles straight north, as the crow flies.

"But it is through a badland country," Emmons added, "which is so difficult to traverse it is impossible to say how long it will take to get there."

"No matter," King said. J. F. Berry knew no faster way out of this wilderness. "We can certainly make better time than he."

King told Emmons to take the camp crew and pack mules back to Fort Bridger, "while I go directly to the head men in this concern at San Francisco, and make them expose this fraud."

This was even bigger than the nation's economy, or the fact that lots of people were about to lose their life savings. Lives were at stake—especially once that Berry fellow started flapping his gums. "Now that the locality is known," King said, "thousands of poor devils will be rushing in here from every quarter, utterly unprepared, and perish by the hundreds in this bleak winter." Leaving at dawn, King and Wilson rode mules all day and through the night. Masterfully navigating the last twenty miles by stars, Wilson led the way directly to Black Buttes. King woke the station agent. He bought two tickets and arranged spots on a boxcar for the mules. He thought about telegraphing the news to San Francisco—but hesitated. Like Harpending, King didn't trust telegraph operators to keep secrets. "No dispatch is safe in their hands," he'd later say. Better to race to Frisco and deliver the bad news himself.

The westbound train rolled into Black Buttes at sunrise.

About sixty-five hours later, Clarence King stood in the hallway of Frisco's Occidental Hotel, pounding on the door of a guest room. No answer. It was past midnight. He pounded some more.

Henry Janin opened the door. Sleepy. Confused.

He let King in, lit a gas lamp. The two friends sat down to talk. King explained how he'd found the diamond field and what he'd discovered there. Janin couldn't believe it. King was sympathetic. The swindlers had clearly invested a fortune in real gems and buried them over an impressive amount of land. They'd also picked a good spot for their fake mine, King said. The area's sandstone formations resembled descriptions of diamondiferous areas in Brazil and southern Africa. Janin had made an understandable mistake.

The conversation lasted all night. Finally Janin was convinced.

Early the next morning, he arranged an emergency diamond company meeting in William Ralston's office at the Bank of California. When Harpending and Roberts arrived, they saw that Janin's eyes were bloodshot. The engineer appeared badly shaken. What could this mean?

Janin introduced Clarence King. The geologist was known to all by reputation. Reading aloud from a report he'd dashed off that morning, King got right to the heartbreaking point.

"I have hastened to San Francisco," he said, "to lay before you the startling fact that the new diamond fields on which are based such large investments and such brilliant hope are utterly valueless, and yourselves and your engineer, Mr. Henry Janin, the victims of an unparalleled fraud."

The room went silent.

King spread a sample of gems from the mine on an office table. He told the investors about the thorough scientific tests he and his men had conducted. He insisted that news of the hoax be made public immediately.

"They were astonished," he'd later say of the investors' reaction, "and thrown into utter consternation."

Harpending's recollection was similar. King's words, he said, "caused a wild excitement among the officers of the company."

The news was devastating. Humiliating. Horrifying. Harpending, Roberts, and the others had been about to put one hundred thousand shares of stock on sale at $100 each—and the price was expected to soar far higher once trading began.

One of the investors suggested that perhaps King might

keep his discovery quiet for a few days. The company could make sure it was in the geologist's financial interest to do so.

Were they offering King a bribe? Hoping to unload some stock before news of the fraud got out?

Outraged, King roared, "There is not money enough in the Bank of California to make me delay the publication a single hour!"

26

THE WILD EAST, PART 2

That same week, on the other side of the country, a very different sort of crime was committed in Rochester, New York.

Susan B. Anthony voted in the presidential election of 1872.

Doesn't sound like much of a crime? Well, women were not permitted to vote in New York. Or in any state. Anthony was charged with casting a ballot in a federal election "without having a lawful right so to vote."

A young man in a top hat and gloves came to Anthony's home, introducing himself as a deputy marshal. She showed him into the parlor. The deputy was visibly uncomfortable. He tried making small talk about the weather. Anthony was no help. Finally, the young man got to the reason for his visit.

"To arrest you," he said.

Anthony was annoyed by the casual, almost gentle way he said this. "Is that the way you arrest men?" she asked.

"No."

"Then I demand that I should be arrested properly."

She held out her hands, waiting to be handcuffed.

The flustered deputy declined to cuff her. He led Anthony to a horse-drawn streetcar and paid her nickel fare to a government building downtown. "Well," she'd later comment, "that was the first cent's worth I ever had from Uncle Sam."

News of Anthony's arrest spread by telegraph, showing up in newspapers around the country. How could it be a crime for a citizen to vote in America? Who was the real criminal in this story? These were questions Americans still needed to debate. The suffrage movement would eventually succeed, with passage of the Nineteenth Amendment—nearly fifty hard-fought years later.

Meanwhile, President Ulysses S. Grant won reelection, gaining over 55 percent of the vote (not counting Susan B. Anthony's vote for Grant, which was thrown out). The losing candidate, Horace Greeley, felt drained from months of campaigning, battered by countless negative articles and cartoons. "I have been assailed so bitterly that I hardly knew whether I was running for president or penitentiary," Greeley told a friend. "Well, I am used up." He died later that month. It's the only time in American history that a major-party candidate died after election day but *before* Congress officially certified the electoral vote.

All this drama made for big stories in the press, of course.

As did the news about to break on the West Coast.

27

BEFOOLED

Clarence King had vowed he would not remain silent "a single hour!"

Yet that evening's editions of Frisco newspapers had nothing about his discovery of the diamond hoax. Nothing in the next morning's papers, either. In fact, word on the street was that King had secretly left town again—with Henry Janin, the noted mining engineer.

"There were rumors that the company was fitting out another expedition," reported the *Chronicle*, "but so carefully and quietly were their arrangements carried out that the party had gone before anything definite could be ascertained."

Another expedition? At this time of year? All of this was clearly diamond related, but what did it mean? People could only guess.

What had actually happened was that Asbury Harpending and the other investors persuaded King to accept a compromise.

The diamond company promised to stop all sales of its stock. In exchange, King agreed to return to the mine to show Henry Janin evidence of the fraud.

King and Janin trekked back to the mine. Janin inspected the site—as an engineer this time, not an investor. This made all the difference. "The ground is absolutely worthless and not diamond-bearing," Janin conceded. "It has been made the field of an ingenious and infamous fraud."

In summary, he said, "I was befooled."

Samuel Emmons reached Fort Bridger with the Fortieth Parallel Survey team's pack mules. He was disturbed to hear that J. F. Berry, the nosy jeweler, had beaten him to the fort. Berry had shown off real diamonds he'd found—failing to mention anything about the mine being a massive hoax. By the time Emmons got to Fort Bridger, many of the soldiers were gearing up to race to the diamond field.

The geologist tried to dissuade them. "It was like talking to stones to try to convince men in this state of excitement," Emmons recalled. "Two army officers started out the day after I arrived, in spite of what I told them."

Berry turned up next in Salt Lake City, proudly announcing he'd been to the famous diamond mine. Unlike others, he proved it by showing claim notices he'd taken from the site. He also had a pocketful of genuine rough gems.

"The people were wild about it," Berry said. They offered him $100,000 to share the location. Resisting this tempting offer, Berry hopped on a train to Frisco.

A reporter cornered him on the train, asking, "What do you think of the discovery? Is it as rich and extensive as we have been told?"

Berry chuckled. "Well, I'm not prepared to say much about that tonight." The jeweler implied that he had friends in Frisco who might want to buy or sell diamond stock, based on what he knew. "You'll get the whole story on Monday," he said, "and I tell you there will be some of the tallest squirming that you ever saw."

"You mean among the stockholders?" asked the reporter.

"Yes."

Remember Mike Gray's decoy expedition? They were still out there!

As winter set in, with no idea of what was happening in Frisco, the diamond hunters found themselves trapped in a two-thousand-foot-deep canyon somewhere in Arizona. Even Gray and Jones were utterly lost. Near starvation, the men spoke openly of shooting their leaders. The group was saved by a Navajo man who guided them out of the canyon and pointed the way to Fort Defiance, the nearest army base.

Months after leaving San Francisco, the searchers staggered into Defiance in a ferocious snowstorm. By this point, they realized they'd been misled in some way but had no idea why. One of the party, a doctor from Frisco, cocked his rifle.

"Men, we have been deceived," he said. "I will kill Jones if you say the word."

The blood drained from Jones's face. He shook with fear.

But most of the guys didn't actually want to murder anyone. They did the next best thing: they kicked their guide out of the fort and into the blizzard.

And as if this story needs one more strange twist, here's a good one.

While Clarence King and Henry Janin were on their way back to San Francisco with terrible news for diamond investors, Alfred Rubery showed up in Kentucky. The one-time pirate from England told people he was a tourist and particularly eager to see Kentucky's famous Mammoth Cave.

In fact, he went to Elizabethtown and found his way to Philip and Mary Arnold's farm.

"I have come to see you," Rubery told Arnold. "Harpending said you would send back some money to him."

Arnold was hesitant, Rubery would later testify. He'd really rather keep all of his money. Eventually, Arnold agreed to hand over nearly $200,000. Rubery carried the cash back to Frisco by train. Harpending met Rubery outside the San Francisco ferry

house. In the privacy of Harpending's carriage, Rubery handed over the money.

Hold on—*What?*

This suspicious episode has never been fully explained. Why would Arnold part with this absolutely astounding sum? Why give it to Harpending? Why at that particular moment?

When the diamond hoax was finally exposed, many would accuse Harpending (and his pal Rubery) of being in on the scam from the start. The plotters, some said, were simply splitting up the take from their successful crime.

Harpending vehemently denied he was anything other than a victim of the devilish caper. "Up to that moment," he insisted, "I had no suspicion of anything improper connected with the diamond scheme."

There's another possible explanation for the $200,000 handoff—probably the most likely one, given this cast of characters. By this point, Harpending realized he'd been scammed. Maybe he'd even begun to suspect it months before. He sent Rubery to Kentucky to confront Arnold. The message to Arnold was, basically: *Okay, congrats, you got me. Now hand over part of your profit, and I'll go easy on you when all of this explodes.*

Which was definitely about to happen.

On the night of Sunday, November 24, Clarence King and Henry Janin returned to San Francisco—and were spotted right away by reporters. King and Janin had been able to keep the true purpose of their journey secret so far. Now they were ready to talk.

28

SALTED!

The shocking news broke the next day. The *San Francisco Chronicle*, which had been covering the country's diamond fever since it erupted, declared:

"SALTED!"

Then followed a stack of additional headlines—for a story this big, the editors could hardly limit themselves to just one or two:

THE DIAMOND BUBBLE BURSTS

THE MOST GIGANTIC SWINDLE ON RECORD

THE MONEY KINGS OF CALIFORNIA
TAKEN IN AND DONE FOR

THE SWINDLERS CARRY OFF OVER HALF A MILLION OF DOLLARS

AFRICAN DIAMONDS USED IN THE SALTING PROCESS

THE STORY OF THE PURCHASE OF STONES IN LONDON PROBABLY TRUE

"The beautiful diamond dream is dispelled," began the *Chronicle* article. "The great diamond discovery assumes the disagreeable aspect of a gigantic deeply-laid fraud."

Newspapers all over the country spent days covering the shocking story. Papers printed detailed accounts of the two-year diamond saga, along with reports of Clarence King's scientific proof of the hoax. Dr. Charles Cleveland, who'd been on the Roberts-Rubery expedition to the mine, offered his own recap: "This was one of the most bare-faced, reckless, courageous, bold, ingenious, premeditated, carefully planned, deliberate, time-serving, colossal frauds ever known in the history of man."

Well said, Doctor.

Or was it?

As the story of the diamond hoax spread to New York, London, and beyond, some refused to believe it. What if the story of the hoax was itself a hoax? Maybe, as one Wyoming miner suggested, the diamond company was worried about people rushing onto their claim. So they cooked up this fake story as a decoy "to prevent parties from prospecting in the right locality."

Another part of the reaction was relief—Americans had narrowly escaped financial disaster. Investors and banks had been about to pour millions into stocks that would prove to be worthless. "It would have caused a catastrophe almost without parallel in the civilized world," Asbury Harpending said. Yes, Harpending was prone to exaggeration. But there would have been a huge and painful crash if the hoax had not been exposed just in time.

Clarence King was the hero of the hour. King and his team showed the world the superpowers of science—not only to explain nature, but even to overpower greed and lies. At thirty years old, the "King of Diamonds," as he was now known, was suddenly a national celebrity. "Fortunately for the good name of San Francisco," declared the editors of the city's *Morning Bulletin*, "there was one cool-headed man of scientific education who esteemed it his duty to investigate the matter in the only right way."

Or, as the *Chronicle* put it: "We have escaped, thanks to God and CLARENCE KING."

29

THE CHIEF SALTER

All of a sudden, reporters couldn't find anyone in Frisco who owned diamond stock.

"Never had any," one broker said.

"I sold out a month ago," said another.

That's typical of scam stories. The moment the scam is exposed, lots of people claim they suspected it all along. Others focus on placing the blame. For the diamond company officials, this made life mighty uncomfortable.

"Roberts and Harpending," reported the *Chronicle*, "are today objects of curious suspicion, to say the least."

People pointed and laughed, shouted insults and nasty jokes. William Lent's hair turned a shade grayer overnight, reporters observed. George Roberts scurried between buildings like a frightened mouse. The angriest glares fell on Asbury Harpending. Who could forget that the man had once been a pirate and a traitor? Harpending walked the streets with his cane clutched in a tight fist, his usual confidence visibly shaken.

"The late diamond millionaires, who had been rather chesty," he confessed, "presented a sad spectacle on the street."

Losing a fortune overnight will do that.

William Ralston, founder of the Bank of California, was out $225,000. In an impressive move, he promised to personally reimburse anyone he'd advised to buy diamond company stock.

George Roberts didn't have that kind of cash. Or any cash. He'd lost about $200,000, and most of that was borrowed. Deeper in debt than ever, Roberts vowed to find some way to pay back the investors who'd supported him.

Harpending, by his own accounting, lost more than anyone. This was probably true—if you don't count the $200,000 he'd secretly collected from Philip Arnold. Luckily for Harpending, the story of this payment did not become public until two years later.

Henry Janin had some serious explaining to do.

How could the country's most trusted mining engineer, with years of experience, be so utterly and disastrously wrong? An embarrassed Janin set out to answer this question in a published report titled *A Brief Statement of My Part in the Unfortunate Diamond Affair*.

One of Janin's key points was that lots of smart people were tricked. "It is too often forgotten," he wrote, "that I was not alone in my mistake, but that the fraud was so well planned as to deceive others as well as myself."

Also, Janin pointed out, his first inspection of the mine was shorter than he'd have liked. He'd wanted to stay longer and make a more detailed study of the diamond field, but Harpending was eager to get back to the city. "Had I been allowed more time, as I desired, in which to make my investigation, it is probable that I would have detected the fraud."

Even the great Clarence King was fooled at first, noted Janin.

Thinking back on his time at the mine, Janin recalled Philip Arnold being especially helpful with the backbreaking work of panning for diamonds. This took on a new meaning now. Had Arnold slipped a few particularly exciting gems into the pan, wanting Janin to feel the thrill of finding these valuable stones?

"It is true that I made a profit of $30,000 by the sale of stock," Janin admitted. He wanted it publicly known that he had already donated the cash to those who'd lost money on the mine.

Does all of this really explain Janin's massive mistake? Yes, if you keep in mind:

1. When Janin was hired, he did not believe that serious people like the lawyer Samuel Barlow and the banker William Ralston would be mixed up in a scam. So he began with the assumption that the diamond mine was real. This clouded his judgment from the start.
2. Janin did not know what diamond fields looked like. Few people in the country did. But he didn't want to admit his ignorance. This is a dangerous weakness, and common.
3. Anything seemed possible in the West. People had found fortunes in gold and silver. Why not diamonds?
4. Remember rule #1 for pulling scams: To fool people, tell them what they want to hear. Janin was a smart guy. But he owned stock in the mine before he inspected it. He took pride in being the first engineer to examine it. He *wanted* it to be real.

"Well, who is the chief salter?"

That was the new question on the streets of Frisco.

It was clear that Philip Arnold and John Slack did the actual salting. But had they acted alone?

The diamond company opened its own investigation, hiring private detectives and calling witnesses to give testimony. A man named J. B. Cooper came forward with an interesting story. Cooper had been Phil Arnold's boss at a Frisco diamond drill company years before. It was while working there, Cooper testified, that Arnold got the idea of salting a diamond mine. That first bag of diamonds, the one Arnold and Slack brought into George Roberts's office late one night in 1870—those rough gems had come from the diamond company's workroom. The cousins purposely picked George Roberts as their first sucker. They knew Roberts was desperate for a big score. Knew he couldn't keep a secret. Knew he'd help them hook bigger fish.

Cooper's tale, and his generally shifty manner, made people suspect he'd been in on the hoax. Had he perhaps advised Arnold on the plan? Had he helped Arnold steal diamonds from the factory to make up that first tempting bundle? Was he now bitter that he hadn't seen any of the profits? Maybe, but his story made sense. It fit with the known facts.

That still left the "chief salter" question. Many newspapers argued that Slack and Arnold could not have pulled off the scam of the century alone. The Kentucky bunco artists simply didn't have the brains to fool so many smart and successful people—that was the theory.

Unless everyone was underestimating Slack and Arnold. Was their whole country-bumpkin image just a clever act? Harpending thought so. The cousins were far smarter than people realized. Talented too. "Both of them had the dramatic gift highly developed," Harpending said. "On the stage they might have made the most famous actors of any time."

This did not make folks stop wondering about Harpending's role in the hoax.

In any case, it seemed clear that Arnold and Slack were guilty. A San Francisco grand jury brought criminal charges against the cousins. William Ralston launched a nationwide search for the salters.

There was absolutely no trace of John Slack.

Philip Arnold was easy to find. He was in Kentucky with Mary and their children, openly strutting the streets of Elizabethtown. Arnold knew this day would come. He had his plan prepared.

He denied everything.

30

THE FEVER BREAKS

"I see by the papers that Arnold and Slack are to be prosecuted," Philip Arnold wrote to his one-time friends at the San Francisco and New York Mining and Commercial Company. "I have employed counsel myself—a good Henry rifle—and I am likely to open my case any day on California Street."

In addition to threatening to shoot his accusers, Arnold insisted he and his cousin were innocent as newborn babes.

"We discovered diamonds and reported the fact to Roberts on our return to San Francisco in November 1870," Arnold explained in a long letter published in the Louisville *Courier-Journal*. He and Slack found the stones atop that mesa on the Colorado-Wyoming border. Had someone salted the field? That was news to Arnold. Must have happened before he got there.

Besides, he led Henry Janin to the mine, didn't he? And Janin declared it diamondiferous, hadn't he?

"I would like to ask any sane man how the ground could have been 'salted' so as to mislead and deceive so many men," Arnold wrote, "they being experts themselves, and especially Janin, one of the shrewdest, smartest men in California on mines."

Janin was now claiming that Arnold told him where to dig. Well, why did Janin listen if it was such bad advice? Why were the big shots who hired Janin so easily duped? It was all absurd. "I could give reasons 'as thick as blackberries,'" Arnold wrote, "but I am tired of making plain what is already 'as plain as the nose on a man's face.'" Rich and powerful men had been humiliated. They needed a scapegoat, and they chose Philip Arnold.

Interestingly, he went out of his way to clear Asbury Harpending of any guilt: "As to Harpending being a confederate of mine in salting, I will say I never salted, and had no confederate."

Arnold continued to insist that he believed the diamond field was real. In fact, he let everyone know he'd be returning in the spring, this time with fifty men. In his letter to the diamond company in Frisco, he added a warning to his former partners: "If I catch any of your kid glove gentry about there, I'll blow the stuffing out of them."

It's not likely that anyone believed Arnold's protests of innocence. Still, he became a bit of a folk hero in his hometown.

Kentucky papers referred to him as "Arnold of diamond fame," the man who'd beaten elite money men at their own greedy game. "If the two men have committed fraud," the Louisville *Courier-Journal* quoted local citizens saying of Arnold and Slack, "they have only been successful in out-Yankeeing the Yankees."

And it was increasingly obvious that Arnold *had* committed fraud. Detectives in London showed his photograph to jewelers. They identified Arnold as "Aundle," the mysterious American who'd bought bags of rough stones on two separate trips to the city.

Back in Frisco, diamond fever faded fast. A street vendor tried hawking "Original Diamond Tooth Paste," implying his product was made with genuine diamond dust. Aside from the dubious wisdom of scrubbing one's teeth with the world's hardest mineral, the poor guy's timing was terrible. "There were but few purchasers," noted the *Chronicle*, "no one seeming to care for diamonds in any way, shape or form."

In the nation's capital, news broke that Representative Benjamin Butler owned one thousand shares of the now worthless diamond stock—taken in exchange for amending the recent mining law. The whiskered politician was yet another person who wished the diamond hoax story would just go away.

Even the charges against Slack and Arnold quietly faded to

nothing. Powerful figures in San Francisco wanted no part of a public trial; better to just forget the whole disagreeable drama. Asbury Harpending used his influence to help make sure no attempt was made to arrest the cousins and haul them back to California.

Was this part of Harpending's secret agreement with Philip Arnold? Seems likely.

One of the major investors, William Lent, refused to let go. Lent traveled to Hardin County, Kentucky, and brought a civil suit against Phil and Mary Arnold, demanding damages of $350,000.

"I never sold one dollar's worth of property to Lent," Arnold fired back, "nor have I ever had any contact with him."

It's true that Arnold never dealt directly with Lent. Still, to be safe, he disappeared from Elizabethtown. If Mary knew where he was hiding, she wasn't talking.

Meanwhile, a county sheriff named W. D. Wood drove a wagon to the Arnold home. Lawyers for both sides followed. Sheriff Wood walked to the big safe in the house and demanded it be opened. Mary Arnold pointed out that the family's property was in her name. Lent knew this, which is why he brought his suit against both Mary and Phil. The safe was opened, its contents carefully cataloged. There was over $250,000 in cash,

railroad bonds, and gold coins. Also valuable silverware and a small fortune in jewelry.

Sheriff Wood hauled it all away, along with the Arnolds' furniture, a two-horse carriage, and twelve stacks of hay. Everything was to be held by the county until the trial was settled.

But the trial never happened. Asbury Harpending appeared in Elizabethtown and helped negotiate a deal between Lent and the Arnolds. Once again, he succeeded in keeping anyone from digging too deeply into the story.

Philip and Mary—while admitting no guilt—agreed to settle the case out of court by paying William Lent the stunning sum of $150,000.

"I did not owe the above-named gentlemen one cent," Philip Arnold told reporters in April 1873, "but I paid the money to purchase my peace and to get loose from this most powerful and world-renowned ring."

William Lent went home satisfied. Sheriff Wood returned Mary and Phil's property. Of the $550,000 Arnold had been paid by diamond company investors, he and Mary still had about $200,000—they were still multimillionaires by today's standards.

And besides, for Philip "of diamond fame" Arnold, the next big strike was always just around the corner.

In fact, barely two years after walking into George Roberts's office with a bag of diamonds, Phil told a few close friends that he'd secretly been prospecting near his home and had made an amazing find. A writer in Louisville got wind of the story, which showed up in newspapers all around the country. "Privately," the article reported, "Arnold says that he has discovered silver mines in Kentucky worth three hundred millions."

What do you think?

Would you buy a share?

EPILOGUE

PRETTY STONES

Philip Arnold had not, in fact, found a fabulous silver mine.

I know. You're shocked.

As attention on the diamond hoax dwindled, Arnold tried yet again to settle into life as a gentleman of wealth and leisure. He added five hundred acres to the family estate and bought Thoroughbred horses. He invested in a new office building named the Gilded Age, which still stands in Elizabethtown today. William McCague, a young boy in the early 1870s, would never forget seeing Arnold swagger around town. "Vain, overbearing, boastful," McCague said of Arnold, "with a toothpick in his mouth and his chest stuck out so that everybody could see a massive gold chain."

Arnold even became a partner in a bank. People don't change, though. Not really. Restless, easily bored, he could never be satisfied with the life of a dignified banker. Pretty soon, a dispute with a rival escalated into a showdown straight out of the Wild West.

The trouble began when Harry Holdsworth, who worked for another bank, started telling half-true tales of Arnold's shady past. "Arnold made what money he had by salting mines in Arizona with diamonds," Holdsworth wrote to a friend. "He was arrested and laid in jail for some time . . . and has since been enjoying his ill-gotten gains."

Arnold learned of the letter. He sued Holdsworth for libel.

But he decided not to wait for the ruling of the court.

Late on the afternoon of August 15, 1878, Arnold was drinking with a friend in Lott's saloon. Holdsworth walked in, stepped to the bar, and ordered a beer.

Arnold strode to Holdsworth, said, "You have done me a mortal injury"—and tossed his enemy to the wood plank floor. Lott, the saloonkeeper, tried to hold Arnold back.

"If you touch me," Arnold snarled, "I will kill you!"

He leapt onto the fallen banker, punching him again and again. Someone ran for the marshal, who finally broke up the brawl. Holdsworth staggered to his bank, washed the blood off his face, grabbed a shotgun stored behind the bank's counter, and strode back toward Lott's saloon.

It was a scene from a Western movie—about twenty years before movies were invented. People watched from sidewalks and windows. According to witnesses, Arnold was now standing in front of the saloon.

Seeing Holdsworth, someone shouted, "There he comes!"

Arnold spun, spotted the armed banker, and pulled out a

revolver. He fired twice, shattering a store window across the street.

Holdsworth lifted the barrel of his shotgun and let loose, sending a swarm of buckshot into Arnold's chest and shoulder. Arnold fell to the street, blood soaking through his shirt. Friends carried him home, where a doctor pronounced the wounds serious but probably not life-threatening.

Early the next year, still not fully recovered from the shootout, Arnold fell ill with pneumonia. He died at the age of just forty-nine. Even with the chaos he brought to town, the adventurous miner was fondly remembered. "The funeral of Philip Arnold yesterday was the largest ever seen in Elizabethtown," reported the Louisville *Courier-Journal*. Several businesses were closed, and the county court adjourned early in honor of his memory.

Mary Arnold lived another twenty-five years—"one of the best known and most highly respected women of this city," declared a local newspaper. Before she passed away in 1904, Mary arranged for each of her four children to get $10,000, an even division of every cent she owned. Some folks in town remembered how rich the Arnolds had once been and simply refused to believe there wasn't more stashed away somewhere.

If there was, it has never been found.

"To this day tradition persists that Arnold buried some of his diamonds in the basement of his mansion and that they are still there!" Bruce A. Woodard wrote in a book on the diamond hoax published in 1967. "Certain susceptible people have taken this seriously and have dug up the basement."

John Slack, Arnold's silent sidekick, was never seen again by any of his old mining pals. Only decades later, long after his death, did researchers find his trail.

After his bitter parting with Alfred Rubery at the diamond field, Slack took a train to St. Louis and found work as a coffin maker. He rose to the position of president of the St. Louis Coffin and Manufacturing Company.

A country boy at heart, Slack returned to his beloved Southwest. He bought a cabin near the mining town of White Oaks, New Mexico, where he earned money making coffins and working as the town undertaker. In 1887, when Slack was in his mid-sixties, he applied for a pension as a veteran of the Mexican-American War. He received these payments for the last nine years of his life.

What happened to his $100,000 haul from the diamond

hoax? That's not clear. He must have lived on some of it in retirement—and may have given a lot of it away. "He was always honest and just," said John Slack's obituary in the *White Oaks Eagle*, "generous to those who gained his ready sympathy and confidence."

Slack left no will. The property he left behind was worth $1,611.14, mostly in the form of his modest house and his carpentry tools.

George Roberts did what he'd always done since joining the Gold Rush as a young man—he went out looking for the next big thing. One of the expeditions he outfitted found a valuable borax mine in Death Valley, California. Slowly, Roberts got back on his feet.

The search for fortune led Roberts to South America, Russia, and Alaska. He did okay, but he never struck it rich. When Roberts died at the age of seventy-three, he was remembered fondly. "Roberts was a man of charming manner," wrote one Frisco paper, "and his invariable kind-heartedness won him innumerable friends."

None of the obituaries mentioned anything about his role in the infamous Great Diamond Hoax. Which, I'm sure, is how Roberts would have wanted it.

Clarence King was one of the few people to come out of the diamond hoax looking good. The celebrity geologist (how often do you say that?) also became a famous author with the publication of *Mountaineering in the Sierra Nevada*, considered an adventure classic to this day.

In the book, King describes a daring trek up Mount Whitney—at 14,505 feet, it's the tallest peak in the United States outside of Alaska. King engraved his name on a silver half-dollar and lodged it between rocks on the summit.

And then realized, a year after his book was published, that he'd climbed the wrong mountain.

He'd actually been atop Mount Langley, at 14,033 feet. Well, it was an easy mistake to make in those days, before accurate maps. Before King helped make them. He went back and climbed Whitney.

If King's life of science and exploration was a great success, his personal life was, well, a lot more complex. This seeker of truth lived a hoax of his own making.

In 1888, in New York, King met a woman named Ada Copeland. She was Black. A public relationship between a white man and a Black woman would have been controversial—illegal in most states. King's response to this ugly racism was questionable at best. He invented a false identity for himself: a light-skinned Black railroad porter named James Todd.

Copeland believed the story, or played along with it. She and "Todd" married and lived together in Brooklyn, where they raised five children. King lived a double life for thirteen years. As Clarence King, he continued his travels and writing, entertaining crowds with riveting tales of outdoor adventures. In Brooklyn, he was a family man named James Todd.

In 1901, suffering from tuberculosis, King wrote a letter to his wife explaining everything he'd done. He died in Arizona at the age of fifty-nine.

Could the Great Diamond Hoax happen again today?

Well, scams are certainly as common now as ever. In one infamous example, an American financier named Bernie Madoff promised investors sky-high returns. But when people gave him money to invest, Madoff just kept it. He created fake records, tricking investors into believing they were earning huge profits. The scam came crashing down when the stock market fell in 2008. People rushed to get their money out—and Madoff didn't have it. He died in jail in 2021.

And of course, we all have to be wary of internet scams. Crooks try to get our personal information by pretending to be a bank, a credit card company, or a down-on-his-luck prince who desperately needs to get millions out of his country. He'll happily transfer his wealth to your account—he just needs your account number. Scammers even use AI to personalize their pitches. I get numerous emails telling me what a fabulous writer I am, with ridiculously over-the-top compliments on my books. If I just click their link, they'll make me as rich and famous as I deserve to be!

If it sounds too good to be true, it is. It's likely a lie or illegal. Or both.

All of that said, the Diamond Hoax could only have happened when it did, in the early 1870s. Vast parts of the country were still not mapped. Americans believed that anything could be out there. And keep in mind, the transcontinental railroad was completed in 1869, just a year before Arnold and Slack launched their scheme. They were able to cross the country in only a week, allowing them to get from Frisco to London and back in under two months. Such rapid travel was new; people weren't used to it yet. When the cousins went out to their mine and returned about six weeks later, who would even imagine they'd actually been across the Atlantic Ocean to buy rough diamonds?

Finally, there were no experienced diamond experts in the United States. No one in America knew how to cut and polish rough diamonds—or even how to accurately value them. Arnold knew this, thanks to his studies at the drill company in Frisco.

Today, with modern tools and training, jewelers can assess diamonds in seconds. The diamond industry has even begun creating digital records of where individual rough diamonds were mined, tracking them as they're cut and sold, so buyers can know the full story of their own particular gem.

Also, we now know where diamonds are—and where they're not. They're not in the Rocky Mountains, or anywhere out west. The one spot in the United States where you can experience the thrill of exploring a genuine diamond field is Crater of Diamonds State Park in Arkansas. And you really can unearth brilliants there, if you're lucky—visitors have found more than thirty-five thousand diamonds in this field since it became a park in 1972.

What about Slack and Arnold's diamond field—the spot they chose for their salted mine?

When the hoax was exposed, most of the gems were still buried out there—genuine uncut diamonds and rubies that had cost the scammers tens of thousands of bucks. The following spring, in May 1873, the *Denver Tribune* cited "certain reliable information" that Philip Arnold had been seen in the West. "He was very reticent about his business and the object of his trip," reported the paper, "but the presumption is he has gone to gather up what is left of his great 'salt.'"

We don't know if this information was actually reliable. We do know that over the years, many people tried to locate the site. A few succeeded. In the early 1970s, a hundred years after the diamond hoax, a geologist named Lowell S. Hilpert not only found the site but recovered some real diamonds. "After several visits," he wrote, "I managed to gather a small but fairly representative sample."

It's likely that diamonds are still buried out there. The field is in an incredibly remote spot along the Colorado-Wyoming border, fifty miles from the nearest town, and several miles off the closest road. The route from the road to the windy mesa is unmarked and brutally rugged.

I know. I've been there.

Anyway, the general area is easy to find online. Just search the northwest corner of Colorado for a mountain called Diamond Peak.

"Of all who were in any material way connected with the historic incident—and there were many—I alone survive."

So wrote **Asbury Harpending** in 1913. By then in his mid-seventies, he'd decided to pen his memoir, modestly titled *The Great Diamond Hoax and Other Stirring Incidents in the Life of Asbury Harpending*.

The book overflows with the adventures of a teenage miner, a rebel pirate, a daring investor. Harpending had many setbacks, but the period of time right after the exposure of the diamond hoax was the most challenging. "I felt crushed beneath the burden of vague suspicion," he wrote, "became disgusted with life in general."

No one outright charged Harpending with being involved in the hoax. But nasty whispers followed him. Mistrust hung above him like fog. His beloved Frisco became, as he put it, "intolerable."

Harpending sold his city real estate, pocketing over a million dollars—and that's 1870s dollars. Actually, he insisted, the fact he owned such valuable buildings was good evidence of his innocence. He was a man of standing in California. Why risk everything when he was already wealthy? "Does it not seem incredible," he wrote, "that a man situated like myself, full of ambition and with everything to live for, would have engaged in an ignoble plot to fleece his friends and the public, a plot absolutely certain to drag him and all belonging to him through the dust?"

It's a pretty convincing argument.

Although . . . this is the same guy who set out at fifteen to conquer Nicaragua. And who thought piracy sounded fun. You'll have to consider the evidence and come to your own conclusion.

Still just thirty-three years old, Harpending moved back to his boyhood home of Princeton, Kentucky, with his wife and children. He built a mansion with indoor plumbing, a swimming pool, fish ponds, fountains, and a greenhouse for growing California grapes.

And then, just like Phil Arnold, he got bored. As he'd later write, "The role of a Kentucky country gentleman was not to my liking."

The Harpending family left Kentucky in 1876. As with the Arnold home, people have since searched the property for secret passages and hidden treasure. No luck so far.

Harpending invested on Wall Street, backed mines in Mexico and Colombia, and made and lost several more fortunes. "I am an old man now—in years, but not in hope," he wrote in his memoir. "I still have very definite ambitions to pull off one more surprise on the world before the close."

He never quite made it. Harpending was in New York City in 1923, trying to sell shares of a new mining operation, when he died at the age of eighty-three. A prominent obituary in the *San Francisco Chronicle* described Harpending as a "pioneer miner and financier" and "Diamond Hoax victim."

He'd have liked that.

Okay, one last story. The perfect place to end, I think.

While researching this book, I tracked down Asbury Harpending's great-grandson, Ron Pavellas. "My father spoke much of his grandfather," Ron told me. "I can't be sure after all this time, but I had the feeling that Dad thought Asbury was not quite innocent."

When Ron's dad was nine years old, he got the chance to poke around Harpending's home in New York City. This was right after Harpending died. The boy rummaged through a dresser, looking under clothing for anything interesting. In one drawer he found what he would always remember as "pretty stones."

Were these diamonds and rubies from the infamous Great Diamond Hoax? Part of the stash Harpending dramatically dumped on his billiard table half a century before? Were they so important to him that—for whatever reason—he'd kept them with him all these years?

We'll never know. We'll certainly never find them.

The boy walked to the second-story window and slid it open. Just for fun, he tossed the stones into the air and watched them sparkle in the sun.

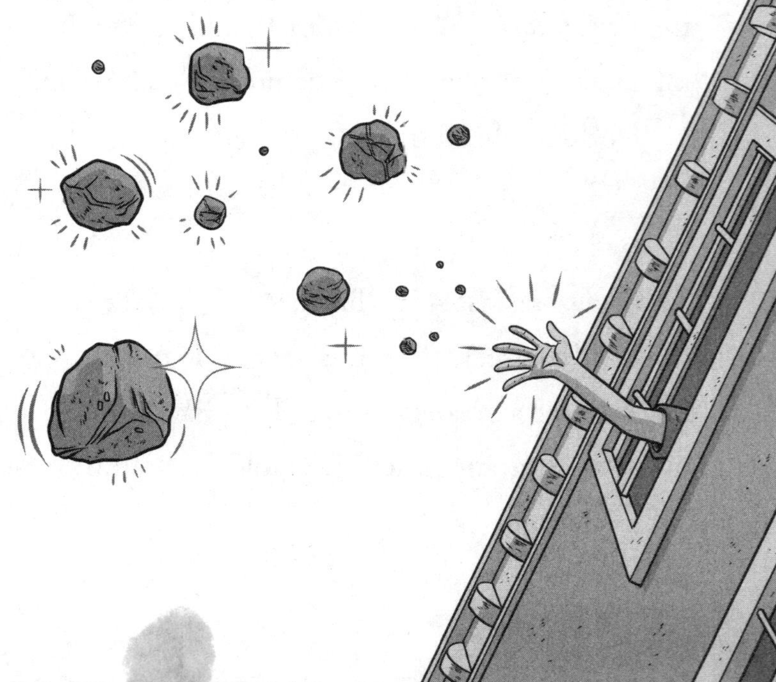

AUTHOR'S NOTE

On a sunny morning in August 2024, my fifteen-year-old son, David, and I waited by the side of a red dirt road near the border of Wyoming and Colorado. To the southwest, rising above the rugged high desert, stood a single pine-green mountain—Diamond Peak.

Right on time, an off-road utility vehicle rolled up. The driver, a rancher named Don Hartley in a baseball cap and sunglasses, leaned out and said, "You must be the fellas." He told us a bit about the local geography, and then uttered maybe the most exciting sentence I've heard in a lifetime of research:

"Wanna go find some diamonds?"

Don drove David in the two-seat UTV. I followed in a rented pickup. Leaving the dirt road behind, we skidded up and down dusty hills and bounced through boulder-filled creek beds, turning several times, following a winding route only Don could see. We finally stopped on top of a mesa—and looked out at Arnold and Slack's diamond field! It was exactly as described by those who were there in 1872: a flat stone surface lined with cracks, covered with pebbles and sand, dotted with shrubs and cactus, windy and chilly even in summer. This was an all-time great research outing, and I'll be forever grateful to Don for guiding us to the legendary spot.

David, on the road to Diamond Peak.

As I tell students all the time, the best part of my job is the detective work. I'd never have found Don without the help of Dick Blust Jr., at the Sweetwater County Historical Museum in Sweetwater, Wyoming. Blust served in law enforcement for more than thirty years and has a vast knowledge of Western history. He generously invited David and me to the museum, shared his thoughts and theories on the diamond hoax, and put me in touch with Don.

Me and Don on the diamond field. How do you find Don? I ain't sayin'.

As always, I relied heavily on the help of librarians and archivists. Thanks to the staff at the American Heritage Center at the University of Wyoming in Laramie, which houses the invaluable Lowell S. Hilpert Papers—thirty-one boxes of maps, articles, and other research materials on the diamond hoax. Frances Kaplan at the California Historical Society went way above and beyond (as librarians so often do) by finding and scanning priceless documents in the Asbury Harpending Papers, including letters between Harpending and George

Roberts, and even Harpending's handwritten cipher dictionaries. Thanks also to the Huntington Library in San Marino, California, which has many key files, including a collection of Clarence King's papers and Henry Janin's pricelessly titled *A Brief Statement of My Part in the Unfortunate Diamond Affair.*

The first reliable nonfiction book on the diamond hoax was *Diamonds in the Salt* by Bruce A. Woodard, published in 1967. You can find the Bruce Albert Woodard Papers in the Western History Collection at the Denver Public Library. I'm also grateful to the Kentucky Archives Center for sharing the records of William Lent's lawsuit against Philip and Mary Arnold. The official records of King's Fortieth Parallel Survey are housed at the National Archives, and many of the files are available online.

Once again, thanks to the Saratoga Springs Public Library, which is just a few blocks from my office and the source of answers to countless research questions.

Thank you to Ron Pavellas (Asbury Harpending's great-grandson!), who shared a mountain of research on the Harpending family, and to Chris Rogers, librarian at the Gemological Institute of America, who sent me rare historical sources on what was known about diamonds in late 1800s. Thanks also to Donald Person, who has offered scientific guidance since my research on *Bomb* many years ago.

I really wanted to include comics in this book, and Connie Hsu, my longtime editor and collaborator, helped figure out how to make it work. Thank you, Connie, for your expert advice on structuring the book and keeping the plot moving fast. Jon Chad has been a family favorite since my kids were young, and I'm thrilled that he agreed to contribute comics and illustrations to this book. Man, can that guy draw!

Thanks to the entire Macmillan team, including Nicolás Ore-Giron, Jen Healey, Sherri Schmidt, Janet Renard, Susan Bishansky, Aurora Parlagreco, Mary Van Akin, Alexandra Quill, Elysse Villalobos, Davina Tomlin, Grace Tyler, Morgan Kane, Tatiana Merced-Zarou, Nicole Schaefer, Shawn Foster, Jen Edwards, Allison Verost, Bess Brasswell, and Jen Besser.

I really did feel the fever!

I'm also very grateful to Steven Malk, Courtney Donovan, and the whole amazing team at Writers House.

As always, thank you to Rachel, Anna, and David for your encouragement and ideas. David was especially helpful this time, traveling with me across remote stretches of Wyoming and Colorado. At the diamond field, we knelt side by side on the mesa, digging in the dirt with gardening trowels we'd bought that morning. I quickly uncovered a small glassy stone and felt a burst of excitement and wonder—a wave of diamond fever! Gathering a few clear pebbles in my palm, I showed them to David.

He took a quick look and said, "Dad, that's quartz."

Yeah, maybe.

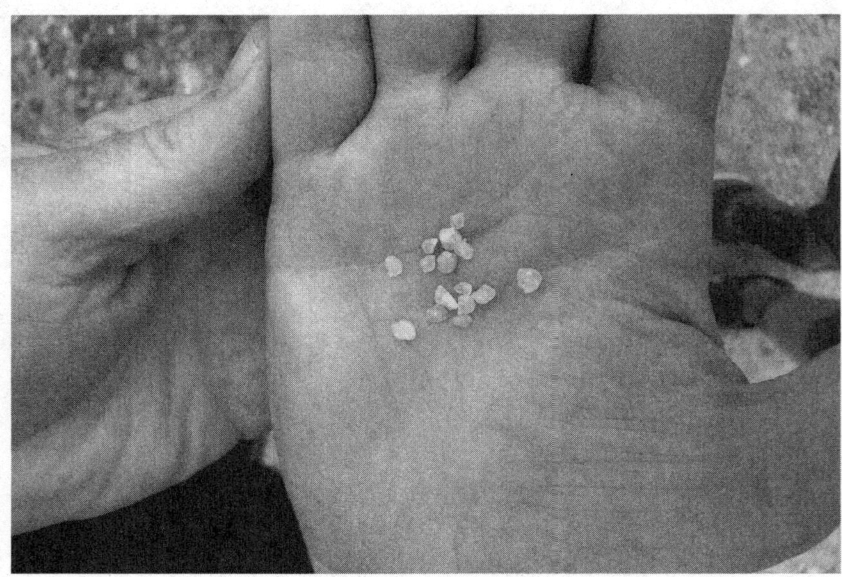

SOURCE NOTES

In the century and a half since the Great Diamond Hoax was exposed in San Francisco, versions of the tale have been told in newspapers and magazines, novels, and televised Westerns. Some accounts stick to known facts; others invent dialogue and details, adding to the mythology of this bizarre crime story. As far as I can tell, no one attempted to research an in-depth nonfiction book on the diamond hoax until the 1960s. Bruce Woodard's *Diamonds in the Salt*, published in 1967, is based on heroic amounts of pre-internet detective work—worth buying just for the source notes. Around the same time, a geologist named Lowell Hilpert gathered thousands of pages of articles, maps, letters, and business records related to the hoax—all of which are available at the University of Wyoming in Laramie.

We're also lucky to have firsthand accounts of the action from the point of view of scammers, victims, and scientists. For those who never wrote books or long articles, you've got to dig a bit deeper—George Roberts's anxious voice, for instance, comes through in private letters to Asbury Harpending. Philip Arnold springs to life in his weird and defiant interviews and letters to newspapers. Should we approach all of these primary sources with a bit of skepticism? Ask ourselves how the speakers' self-interest may have influenced what they chose to say—and to leave out? Sure, always!

PROLOGUE

1 Verdi train robbery sources: "Greatest Highway Robbery on the Pacific Coast!," *Gold Hill (NV) Daily News*, Nov. 5, 1870; "Our Officers Recover Nearly $20,000," *Nevada Territorial Enterprise*, Nov. 12, 1870; Cachinero, "Highwaymen," 72–78; and Renda, "Verdi's Historic Train Heist."

PART 1 COMIC

5 The comics in this book are a combination of my scripts and Jon Chad's masterful art. The comics are nonfiction, and we both relied on written and visual historical sources. Arnold relates the scene in Roberts's office in his letter to the editor in "Philip Arnold's Money," *Courier-Journal* (Louisville, KY), Dec. 16, 1872. Roberts tells Asbury Harpending of the diamond find in a telegram sent on Dec. 1, 1870.

1. THE SECRET

11 "Rough diamonds" and the scene in Roberts's office: Woodard, *Diamonds in the Salt*, 22; Wilkins, *Clarence King*, 168; and Arnold, letter to the editor, in "Philip Arnold's Money," *Courier-Journal* (Louisville, KY), Dec. 16, 1872.

12 "It may not pay to hunt for diamonds": W. A. Goodyear, "The Gravel Hills of Placerville," *Mountain Democrat* (Placerville, CA), Oct. 28, 1871, quoted in *Statistics of Mines and Mining in the States and Territories West of the Rocky Mountains, Being the Fourth Annual Report of Rossiter W. Raymond, U.S. Commissioner of Mining Statistics* [for year ending Dec. 31, 1871] (Washington, D.C., 1873): 27.

2. LUCKY FIND

14 "Are you alone?" and start of Gold Rush: Bancroft, *History of California*, 26–41; Rosen, *Gold!*, 44–46; and Wallentine, "There's a Better Way."

15 George Roberts's background: "Death Closes a Famous Life," *San Francisco Call*, Dec. 25, 1901; and Lescohier, *Gold Giants*, 7, 38.

16 "I am at the end of my tether": Roberts to Harpending, Jan. 15, 1871, Harpending Papers.

16 "I am busted sure": Roberts to Harpending, Jan. 20, 1871.

3. THE PARTNERS

19 Roberts owed Arnold $20,000: *The Mining Journal* (London), Aug. 15, 1874.

19 Philip Arnold's and John Slack's backgrounds: Woodard, *Diamonds in the Salt*, 1–4; Hilpert, "Great Diamond Swindle," 18–25, 48–55; and Lavender, *Nothing Seemed Impossible*, 294–95.

20 "Indian territory": Wilson, *Explorer King*, 238.

21 "Arnold has returned": Roberts to Harpending, Dec. 1, 1870, telegram reprinted in Hilpert, "Great Diamond Swindle," 12.

22 "I have great hopes from this discovery": Roberts to Harpending,

Jan. 4, 1871, telegram reprinted in Hilpert, "Great Diamond Swindle."

23 "Could it really be true": Harpending, *Great Diamond Hoax*, 199.

23 "something that would astonish the world": Two years after the diamond hoax was exposed in the United States, Rubery was involved in a hoax-related case in London, *Rubery v. Grant and Sampson*. Many of the key players gave testimony, and transcripts from the trial in the Court of Exchequer were published in the Law Report of *The Times* of London. This is from the deposition of [Charles W.] Rand in "Rubery v. Grant and Sampson," *The Times*, Dec. 24, 1874.

24 "Personally, I am bored to death": Harpending, 200.

4. THE PIRATES

25 Harpending's background and early adventures: Harpending, *Great Diamond Hoax*, 11–24; and Woodard, *Diamonds in the Salt*, 5–6.

26 Rubery's background: Woodard, 5–6; and Harpending, 65.

27 "High words followed": Harpending, 66.

27 "He admitted that he had some knowledge": Harpending, 69.

27 "Now we're getting somewhere": Harpending, 71.

28 *Chapman* episode sources: Gilbert, "Kentucky Privateers," 256–66; "A Rebel Privateer Fitted Out in This Port," *Daily Alta California* (San Francisco), Mar. 16, 1863; and Harpending, 75–88.

30 "That you, Harpending?" and scene in Alcatraz prison cell: Harpending, 82.

5. CITY IN A HURRY

32 San Francisco city details: Lewis, *This Was San Francisco*, 159–83; Neville, *Fantastic City*, 174–204; Bowles, *Our New West*, 332–61; and Lavender, *Nothing Seemed Impossible*, 200–1.

33 "In walking two blocks": Evans, *À la California*, 132.

34 "I then refused to sell": Arnold, letter to the editor, in "Philip Arnold's Money," *Courier-Journal* (Louisville, KY), Dec. 16, 1872.

35 "Before we close the deal" and Ralston's early involvement: Dickson, *Tales of San Francisco*, 370: Lavender, *Nothing Seemed Impossible*, 301.

35 Slack agrees to sell: Woodard, *Diamonds in the Salt*, 23–24.

35 Mary Arnold's background: Woodard, 7–8; and Hilpert, "Great Diamond Swindle," 20–21.

35 "His life was continually in danger": Answer of Mary E. Arnold, Jan. 18, 1873, in *Lent v. Arnold et al.*

36 Mary got the $20,000: Contract between George Roberts and Mary E. Arnold, in *Lent v. Arnold et al.*

6. THE WILD WEST, PART 2

38 Jesse James's Iowa bank robbery: Smith, "Jesse James," 377–80; and "Another Bank Robbery," *Evening Telegraph* (Philadelphia), June 24,

1871, reprinted from *Lineville (IA) Index*.

38 "If y'all ain't too busy": Smith, "Jesse James," 378.

PART 2 COMIC

41 Diamond history and scientific facts can be found in modern sources—such as Hart, *Diamond*, and Rossi, "How Can Graphite and Diamond Be So Different"—and in books from Slack and Arnold's time, such as Emanuel, *Diamonds and Precious Stones*. To learn more about how diamonds formed and reached the earth's surface, see Smit and Shirey, "Kimberlites."

7. THE COUSINS RETURN

45 "He seemed to take a great interest": "Cooper's Story," *Evening Bulletin* (San Francisco), Dec. 7, 1872.

46 "The first thing to be looked after": "The Diamond—No. 2," *Mining and Scientific Press* 25, no. 7 (Aug. 17, 1872): 97.

46 "Almost all gems conceal their beauties": Emanuel, *Diamonds and Precious Stones*, 4.

48 "Both were travel-strained": Harpending, *Great Diamond Hoax*, 204–5.

8. DAZZLING LIGHT

51 "It seemed" and scene in billiard room: Harpending, *Great Diamond Hoax*, 205.

53 "A peculiar man": Deposition of General Dodge in "Rubery v. Grant and Sampson," *The Times*, Dec. 24, 1874.

53 Slack sells out: Woodard, *Diamonds in the Salt*, 26.

54 "That will settle everything": Ferguson, "Great Diamond Hoax," 7.

55 "Meals! Meals for fifty cents!" and other travel details: Jackson, *Bits of Travel*, 10; Blakemore, "What Was It Like"; and Coolidge, "A Few Hints," 25–31.

9. THE GILDED AGE

59 Scene in Barlow's mansion: Woodard, *Diamonds in the Salt*, 27–28; Harpending, *Great Diamond Hoax*, 208; and Liebling, "American Golconda," 53.

59 "Gentlemen, these are beyond question": Harpending, 208.

61 "The O.K. of Henry Janin": Harpending, 209.

61 "Suppose I go in the spring" and "You might trust these men": "Hon. Wm. M. Lent's Story" in "Eureka," *Evening Bulletin* (San Francisco), Dec. 6, 1872.

62 Arnold makes a deal, putting money in his shirt: Harpending, 210; and deposition of Samuel L. M. Barlow, Jan. 9, 1879, in court records of *Arnold and Polk v. Longshaw and Holdsworth*, Hardin County, KY, quoted in Woodard, 30.

10. LONG WINTER

63 "I am depending on the A. matter": Roberts to Harpending, telegram, Nov. 6, 1871, Harpending Papers.

64 "Money is tight": Roberts to Harpending, telegram, Feb. 26, 1872, Harpending Papers.

64 "Mrs. A. has not heard": Roberts to Harpending, telegram, Feb. 26, 1872, Harpending Papers.

65 Harpending's London expenses: box 1, folder 13, Harpending Papers.

65 "Mr. Arnold arrived here": Roberts to Harpending, telegram, Mar. 18, 1872, Harpending Papers.

66 Butler accepted one thousand shares: "The Great Fraud," *San Francisco Chronicle*, Nov. 27, 1782.

66 Expedition leaves train in Wyoming: Harpending, *Great Diamond Hoax*, 213; and Woodard, *Diamonds in the Salt*, 37.

PART 3 COMIC

69 "The country was wild" and other quotes from journey: Harpending, *Great Diamond Hoax*, 213–14.

72 "Come, Rubery": Henry Janin recalled Rubery finding the first diamond, in his deposition in "Rubery v. Grant and Sampson," *The Times*, Dec. 22, 1874.

73 "That's a diamond": Harpending, 214.

11. HAPPY MOOD

75 "We began to have all kinds of luck" and details of diamond field: Harpending, *Great Diamond Hoax*, 214; and "Janin's Preliminary Report," June 26, 1872, in "The Diamond Mines," *San Francisco Chronicle*, Aug. 6, 1872.

75 "I had not been on the ground": "The Great Salt," *San Francisco Chronicle*, Dec. 6, 1872.

75 "wildly enthusiastic": Harpending, 215.

75 "You may depend upon it" and "the most momentous discovery": Harpending, 214.

77 "Two days' work satisfied Janin": Harpending, 215.

78 "We staked off in a rough way" and "This Rubery rebelled against": Harpending, 216.

78 Rubery $300 a week: "Rubery's Statement" in "The Diamond Swindle," *Evening Bulletin* (San Francisco), Dec. 5, 1872.

79 FOUR AND FIVE IN GREAT QUANTITIES: Harpending to Ralston, telegram, Harpending Papers.

80 Harpending's ciphers: Box 1, folder 9, Harpending Papers.

81 "quarreled very severely": *The Times*, Dec. 24, 1874.

12. WILD SCRAMBLE

82 "While I did not have time enough" and other details from Janin's report: "Janin's Preliminary Report," June 26, 1872, in "The Diamond Mines," *San Francisco Chronicle*, Aug. 6, 1872; Woodard, *Diamonds in the Salt*, 41; and Arnold, letter to the editor, in "Philip Arnold's Money," *Courier-Journal* (Louisville, KY), Dec. 16, 1872.

83 "There was a wild scramble to get on board": Harpending, *Great Diamond Hoax*, 218.

83 "I answered Baron Rothschild": Harpending, 218.

83 "America is a rich land": Liebling, "American Golconda," 59.

84 "If I only had the property back": "Hon. Wm. Lent's Story" in "Eureka," *Evening Bulletin* (San Francisco), Dec. 6, 1872.

84 Arnold accepted his $150,000, plus another $300,000: Woodard, 42–43.

84 "Thus, the decks were cleared": Harpending, 223.

13. DIAMONDS AND SALT

85 Salting stories: Plazak, *Hole in the Ground*, 17–21; Trimble, "Salting a Gold Mine"; Lavender, "How to Salt a Gold Mine"; and Cunningham, "200 Years of Illinois."

87 Slack and Arnold in London: Harpending, *Great Diamond Hoax*, 246–49; L. Keller and Co., letter in "Money-Market and City Intelligence," *The Times*, Aug. 30, 1872; and "Rubery v. Grant and Sampson," *The Times*, Dec. 21 and 24, 1874.

88 "How much for the lot": Harpending, 249.

91 Arnold's take from the scam: Woodard, *Diamonds in the Salt*, 43; and Lavender, *Nothing Seemed Impossible*, 315.

91 Arnold family in Elizabethtown: Hilpert, "Great Diamond Swindle," 18; and Woodard, 121–22.

14. THE WILD EAST

92 President Grant's arrest: Kemp, "Thin Blue Line"; and "Only Policeman Who Ever Arrested a President," *Evening Star* (Washington, D.C.), Sept. 27, 1908.

94 Grant's reelection hopes: Chernow, *Grant*, 739–47.

94 "The excitement over the great discovery": "The Diamond Wonder," *San Francisco Chronicle*, Aug. 2, 1872.

15. CALIFORNIA STREET

95 Diamond display, including "Many enthusiastic expressions": "The Diamond Wonder," *San Francisco Chronicle*, Aug. 2, 1872; "The Diamond Sensation," *San Francisco Chronicle*, Aug. 3, 1872; Woodard, *Diamonds in the Salt*, 47; and Harpending, *Great Diamond Hoax*, 233.

96 "On California Street" and conversations on the street: "The Diamond Wonder," *San Francisco Chronicle*, Aug. 2, 1872; and "The Diamond Sensation," *San Francisco Chronicle*, Aug. 3, 1872.

97 "You bet, I have got the stock": "The Diamond Sensation," *San Francisco Chronicle*, Aug. 3, 1872.

98 "No; there is nothing more": "The Diamond Wonder," *San Francisco Chronicle*, Aug. 2, 1872.

99 "About 1,000 miles to the east": George D. Lyman, *Ralston's Ring: California Plunders the Comstock Lode* (Charles Scribner's Sons, 1937), 191, quoted in Woodard, *Diamonds in the Salt*, 48.

16. THE COUNTRY GENTLEMAN

100 Arnold in Elizabethtown: Josiah M. Ward, "Phil Arnold Beat Up the Wrong Man," *Denver Post Magazine*, Apr. 24, 1921.

101 Arnold agrees to return to the mine: Woodard, *Diamonds in the Salt*, 58.

PART 4 COMIC

104 "There is no bum": William Whitman Bailey to brother, June 30, 1867, Bailey Papers, Huntington Library, San Marino, CA, quoted in William H. Goetzmann, *Exploration and Empire: The Explorer and the Scientist in the Winning of the American West* (Knopf, 1971), 438, quoted in Wilson, *Explorer King*, 192.

104 "Pitch in, my boy": James D. Hague, "Memorabilia," in Century Association, *Clarence King Memoirs*, 402.

106 "I was staggered": King to A. A. Humphreys, Dec. 18, 1867, Records of the Geological Exploration of the Fortieth Parallel.

106 "With him nothing was impossible": Samuel F. Emmons's notes on King for R. W. Raymond, Clarence King Papers, quoted in Wilkins, *Clarence King*, 115.

106 "He came out of the adventure": Private letter of William Brewer in Rossiter W. Raymond, "Biographical Notice," in Century Association, 319.

17. CLARENCE KING

109 "For me the study": Edgar Beecher Bronson, *Reminiscences of a Ranchman* (McClure, 1908), 3, quoted in Wilson, *Explorer King*, 95.

110 "a veritable museum" and childhood details: Emmons, *Biographical Memoir*, 29; and Wilson, *Explorer King*, 27–30.

110 King's journey to California: Moore, *King of the 40th Parallel*, 28–47; and Wilson, *Explorer King*, 61–72.

110 Fortieth Parallel Survey plan: Wilson, *Explorer King*, 180–81; and Moore, 141.

111 "a man of undoubted integrity": Emmons's field notes, "The Diamond Discovery of 1872," R.G. 57, National Archives, quoted in Woodard, *Diamonds in the Salt*, 100.

112 "The summer has been one uninterrupted success": King to A. A. Humphreys, Oct. 28, 1872, Records of the Geological Exploration of the Fortieth Parallel.

18. COMPETING CLAIMS

113 Lloyd MacIntyre hired by Arnold: Tommy Thomas, "E'town Diamonds Fooled Frisco," *Courier-Journal Sunday Magazine* (Louisville, KY), Dec. 10, 1939.

113 "Considerable curiosity": "On the Hunt," *Omaha Daily Bee*, Aug. 1, 1872.

116 "There is a great deal of misery": "The Diamond Fever," *Sacramento Daily Union*, Aug. 7, 1872.

116 "It is becoming well known that Santa Fe": *New Mexican* (Santa Fe), Aug. 22, 1872, p. 1.
117 "The Times will offer a splendid premium": *Daily Denver Times*, Aug. 30, 1872, p. 4.
117 "This is all old to me": C. O. Brown, letter, Aug. 19, 1872, in "Location of the Arizona Diamond Fields," *Daily Alta California* (San Francisco), Sept. 2, 1872.
118 "I am going back": "The Diamond Mines," *San Francisco Chronicle*, Aug. 4, 1872.
118 "Miner is a bilk": "The Diamond Mines," *San Francisco Chronicle*, Aug. 6, 1872.
118 "He had better not call me names": "The Diamond Excitement," *San Francisco Call*, Aug. 7, 1872.

19. TWO ARNOLDS

119 "I am the original discoverer" and other quotes from interview: "Correct History of the Diamond Discovery," *Laramie Daily Sentinel*, Aug. 19, 1872; *Rocky Mountain News*, Aug. 2, 1872.
121 "There are so many people going": "Great Diamond Fields," *Daily Independent*.
121 "I was much surprised" and "I cannot enlighten": "The Diamond Mines," *San Francisco Chronicle*, Aug. 21, 1872.
122 "Denver was, indeed, ablaze": *Denver Tribune*, Feb. 6, 1879, quoted in Woodard, *Diamonds in the Salt*, 67.
123 "On my way up to Santa Fe": "The Diamond Seekers," *San Francisco Chronicle*, Nov. 25, 1872.
123 "It is rumored on the street today": "Rumored Murder," *Daily Bee* (Sacramento, CA), Aug. 3, 1872.

20. TWO EXPEDITIONS

125 Mike Gray expedition sets out, including "Where are you going?": "Lost in the Mountains," *St. Louis Globe-Democrat*, Dec. 17, 1883.
126 "Each man is sworn to secrecy": "By State Telegraph: Third Dispatch," *Sacramento (CA) Daily Union*, Aug. 30, 1872.
126 "Keep quiet": "Lost in the Mountains," *St. Louis Globe-Democrat*.
126 "fierce looking fellows": "The Diamond Question," *Daily Rocky Mountain News* (Denver), Sept. 7, 1872.
126 "Let them go by what route they may": "By State Telegraph," *Sacramento Daily Union*.
127 "Everything was done": Cleveland, "Autobiography," 41.
127 "Gillette, you are looking thin": "An Interview with Colonel Gillette" in "The Diamond Mines," *San Francisco Chronicle*, Oct. 8, 1872.
128 "I hope you will get there": Deposition of Dr. [Charles] Cleveland in "Rubery v. Grant and Sampson," *The Times*, Dec. 24, 1874.
128 "Shall we allow those men" and other journey details: "Lost in the Mountains," *St. Louis Globe-Democrat*.

129 "We are going to the diamond fields" and "We went a very roundabout way": Cross-examination of Rubery in "Rubery v. Grant and Sampson," *The Times*, Dec. 21, 1874.

130 "It's very strange": Cross-examination of Charles Godlove Meyer in "Rubery v. Grant and Sampson," *The Times*, Dec. 24, 1874.

131 "an ordeal of the most wearing": Cleveland, "Autobiography," 41.

131 "When will we reach the diamond fields?": Cleveland, 41.

PART 5 COMIC

133 Arnold's interview in Denver and reporter's commentary: "Diamonds Till You Can't Rest," *Daily Rocky Mountain News*, Sept. 8, 1872. (Yes, the word *'personated* really was used.)

134 "We had ceased to think": "Lost in the Mountains," *St. Louis Globe-Democrat*, Dec. 17, 1883.

135 "I'd scarcely give": Emmons, "Diamond Discovery," 3.

136 London diamond merchant's letter: Pittar, Leverson, and Co., letter in "Money-Market and City Intelligence," *The Times*, Aug. 29, 1872; L. Keller and Co., letter in "Money-Market and City Intelligence," *The Times*, Aug. 30, 1872; and "The Diamond Mystery," *San Francisco Chronicle*, Sept. 20, 1872.

138 Rubery gets lost: Cross-examination of Rubery in "Rubery v. Grant and Sampson," *The Times*, Dec. 21, 1874; and Cleveland, "Autobiography," 41.

21. GLITTER AND FLASH

139 "These are about two or three ounces" and other details of scene in jeweler's shop: "Bitter Disappointment," *San Francisco Chronicle*, Sept. 25, 1872.

140 "This news did not disturb me": "Hon. Wm. H. Lent's Story" in "Eureka," *Evening Bulletin* (San Francisco), Dec. 6, 1872.

141 "This is the place": Deposition of Charles Godlove Meyer in "Rubery v. Grant and Sampson," *The Times*, Dec. 24, 1874.

142 "Roberts turned out the first loaf": "An Interview with Colonel Gillette" in "The Diamond Mines," *San Francisco Chronicle*, Oct. 8, 1872.

143 Emmons and Gardner on the train to California: Emmons, "Diamond Discovery," 4.

22. THE DIAMONDIFEROUS LOCALITY

145 "Very clear fine stones": Emmons, "Diamond Discovery," 4.

146 "the diamondiferous locality": Emmons, "Diamond Discovery," 5.

147 "Where is Roberts?" and conversation on train: "The Diamonds," *San Francisco Chronicle*, Oct. 7, 1872.

148 "Every holder of the company's stock": Harpending, *Great Diamond Hoax*, 229.

148 "If they have been deceived": "The

Diamond Fields," *Evening Bulletin* (San Francisco), Oct. 7, 1872.

23: CARBONIFEROUS FOSSILS

150 "and various other things": Wilson, "Great California Diamond Mines," 292.

150 "The information thus gathered": Emmons, "Diamond Discovery," 6.

150 "Where do you think": Emmons, "Diamond Discovery," 8.

152 "I was certain" and "It would be a blight": Deposition of Clarence King in "Rubery v. Grant and Sampson," *The Times*, Dec. 24, 1874.

152 "carboniferous fossils": Emmons, "Diamond Discovery," 8.

153 "If all the stories and theories": "The Diamond Hunt," *San Francisco Chronicle*, Aug. 10, 1872.

24. FULL BELIEVERS

154 King's team searches for mine: Wilson, "Great California Diamond Mines," 292–93; Emmons, "Diamond Discovery," 9–11; and Wilson, *Explorer King*, 247–48.

156 "It seemed strange": Wilson, "Great California Diamond Mines," 293.

157 "That night we were full believers": Emmons, "Diamond Discovery," 11.

PART 6 COMIC

159 King describes his team's work in a detailed letter to his boss, General A. A. Humphries, Chief of the Army Corps of Engineers, Nov. 27, 1872, and in his deposition in "Rubery v. Grant and Sampson," *The Times*, Dec. 24, 1874. See also Emmons, "Diamond Discovery," 12–14; and Wilson, "Great California Diamond Mines," 293–95.

162 "Found any carats around here?": Emmons, "Diamond Discovery," 14.

25. STARTLING FACTS

163 Berry's arrival and conversation with the team: Emmons, "Diamond Discovery," 14–15.

164 "That man will make mischief" and other campfire quotes: Emmons, "Diamond Discovery," 16.

166 "No dispatch is safe": King to A. A. Humphreys, Nov. 27, 1872, Records of the Geological Exploration of the Fortieth Parallel.

166 King and Janin talk in hotel: Woodard, *Diamonds in the Salt*, 111; and Janin, *Brief Statement*, 6.

167 "I have hastened to San Francisco": Janin reprints King's report to the diamond company in his *Brief Statement*, 7–12.

167 "They were astonished": King to Humphreys, Nov. 27, 1872.

167 "caused a wild excitement": Harpending, *Great Diamond Hoax*, 234.

168 "There is not money enough": Emmons, *Clarence King*, 9.

26. THE WILD EAST, PART 2

169 Anthony arrested for voting: McGreevy, "Susan B. Anthony Was Arrested"; "Woman Suffragists,"

The World (New York), May 7, 1873; copy of commitment and order to U.S. marshal, Dec. 26, 1872, in *United States v. Susan B. Anthony*; and "Female Suffrage," *Rochester (NY) Democrat and Chronicle*, Nov. 30, 1872.

170 "I have been assailed so bitterly": Greeley to Mason W. Tappan, Nov. 8, 1872, quoted in Daugherty, "This Defeated Presidential Candidate."

27. BEFOOLED

171 "There were rumors": "Salted or Not?," *San Francisco Chronicle*, Nov. 24, 1872.

172 "The ground is absolutely worthless": Janin, *Brief Statement*, 13.

172 "It was like talking to stones": Emmons, "Diamond Discovery," 17.

173 "The people were wild about it": "Salted or Not?," *San Francisco Chronicle*.

174 "Men, we have been deceived": "Lost in the Mountains," *St. Louis Globe-Democrat*, Dec. 17, 1883.

174 "I have come to see you": Cross-examination of Rubery in "Rubery v. Grant and Sampson," *The Times*, Dec. 21, 1874.

175 "Up to that moment": Cross-examination of Rubery, *The Times*.

28. SALTED!

177 *San Francisco Chronicle* headlines and story: "SALTED!" *San Francisco Chronicle*, Nov. 25, 1872.

178 "This was one of the most barefaced": Cleveland, "Autobiography," 41–42.

179 "to prevent parties from prospecting": "From Rawlins," *Daily Independent* (Laramie, WY), Dec. 5, 1872.

179 "It would have caused a catastrophe": Harpending, *Great Diamond Hoax*, 230.

179 "Fortunately for the good name of San Francisco": *Morning Bulletin* (San Francisco), editorial, Nov. 27, 1872, quoted in Wilkins, *Clarence King*, 171.

179 "We have escaped": "Diamond Dust Cuts Diamonds," editorial, *San Francisco Chronicle*, Nov. 28, 1872.

29. THE CHIEF SALTER

180 "Never had any," "I sold out," and "Roberts and Harpending": "Unmasked!," *San Francisco Chronicle*, Nov. 26, 1872.

181 "The late diamond millionaires": Harpending, *Great Diamond Hoax*, 242.

181 "It is too often forgotten" and Janin's version of events: Janin, *Brief Statement*, 3–5.

183 "Well, who is the chief salter?": "The Great Fraud," *San Francisco Chronicle*, Nov. 27, 1872.

184 J. B. Cooper's story: "The Great Salt," *San Francisco Chronicle*, Dec. 6, 1872; and "Cooper's Story," *Evening Bulletin* (San Francisco), Dec. 7, 1872.

185 "Both of them had the dramatic gift": Harpending, 245.

30. THE FEVER BREAKS

186 "I see by the papers": Philip Arnold to Diamond Company, in "Arnold

Heard From," *San Francisco Chronicle*, Dec. 12, 1872.

186 "We discovered diamonds" through "As to Harpending": Arnold, letter to the editor, in "Philip Arnold's Money," *Courier-Journal* (Louisville, KY), Dec. 16, 1872.

187 "If I catch any of your kid glove gentry": Arnold to Diamond Company, *San Francisco Chronicle.*

188 Kentucky reaction, including "If the two men have committed fraud": "Philip Arnold's Money," *Courier-Journal.*

188 "There were but few purchasers": "The Great Fraud," *San Francisco Chronicle*, Nov. 27, 1872.

189 "I never sold one dollar's worth": Arnold letter in "Philip Arnold's Money," *Courier-Journal.*

189 Lent-Arnold lawsuit and settlement: Woodard, *Diamonds in the Salt*, 128–30; and records of *Lent v. Arnold et al.*

191 "I did not owe the above-named gentlemen": "Great Diamond Suit," *Courier-Journal* (Louisville, KY), Apr. 4, 1873.

191 "Privately, Arnold says": "Diamond Arnold Denies," *Daily Examiner* (San Francisco), Dec. 16, 1872.

EPILOGUE: PRETTY STONES

192 "Vain, overbearing, boastful": Josiah M. Ward, "Phil Arnold Beat Up the Wrong Man," *Denver Post Magazine*, Apr. 24, 1921.

193 "Arnold made what money he had": Harry N. Holdsworth to Charles Bird, May 3, 1878, in court records of *Arnold and Polk v. Longshaw and Holdsworth*, Hardin County, KY, quoted in Woodard, *Diamonds in the Salt*, 160.

193 "You have done me a mortal injury" and other showdown details: "Elizabethtown," *Courier-Journal* (Louisville, KY), Aug. 29, 1878.

194 "The funeral of Philip Arnold": "Elizabethtown, Ky.," *Courier-Journal* (Louisville, KY), Feb. 12, 1879.

194 "one of the best known": "Hardin County," *Larue County Herald* (KY), May 19, 1904, reprinted from *The Mirror*, Elizabethtown, KY. See also "Death of Mrs. Mary Arnold," *Elizabethtown News*, May 13, 1904.

194 "To this day tradition persists": Woodard, 157.

196 "He was always honest": "An Honored Citizen Gone," *White Oaks Eagle*, July 30, 1896.

196 Value of Slack's estate: Records from the Probate File of John B. Slack, Lincoln County Courthouse, Carrizozo, NM, quoted in Woodard, 172.

196 "Roberts was a man of charming manner": "Death Closes a Famous Life," *San Francisco Call*, Dec. 25, 1901. See also "Obituary Notes," *New York Times*, Dec. 25, 1901. An odd note: George Roberts and Clarence King died on the same day; their obituaries appear on the same page of this edition of the *Times*.

197 King on Mount Whitney: King, *Mountaineering*, 278.

197 Ada Copeland story: Sandweiss,

Passing Strange, 131–57; and Wilson, *Explorer King*, 255–56.

199 Finding diamonds in the United States: Crater of Diamonds State Park, Arkansas State Parks, arkansasstateparks.com/parks/crater-diamonds-state-park.

199 "certain reliable information": *Denver Tribune*, May 24, 1873, quoted in Woodard, 175.

200 "After several visits": Hilpert, "Field Investigation," 317.

200 "Of all who were in any material way" and "I felt crushed": Harpending, *Great Diamond Hoax*, 260.

201 "Does it not seem incredible": Harpending, 258.

202 "The role of a Kentucky gentleman": Harpending, 278.

202 "I am an old man now": Harpending, 283.

202 "Pioneer miner and financier": "Famed State Financier Dies in the East at 83," *San Francisco Chronicle*, Jan. 27, 1923.

203 "My father spoke much of his grandfather" and story from Harpending's great-grandson: email from Ron Pavellas to author, Jan. 15, 2024.

BIBLIOGRAPHY

FIRSTHAND ACCOUNTS

Century Association King Memorial Committee. *Clarence King Memoirs.* G. P. Putnam's Sons, 1904.

Cleveland, Charles Dexter. "Autobiography and Reminiscence of Dr. Charles Dexter Cleveland," San Francisco, 1901. Transcription. Society of California Pioneers Collection of Autobiographies and Reminiscences of Early Pioneers, Online Archive of California. oac.cdlib.org/ark:/13030/kt2489q2gr.

Emmons, Samuel Franklin. *Biographical Memoir of Clarence King, 1842–1901*. Read before the National Academy of Sciences, Apr. 23, 1903. Judd & Detweiler, 1907.

Emmons, Samuel Franklin. *Clarence King: A Memorial. Engineering and Mining Journal*, 1902.

Emmons, Samuel Franklin. "The Diamond Discovery of 1872." Emmons Papers.

Emmons, Samuel Franklin. Diary, Oct. 6, 1872. Box 32. Emmons Papers.

Harpending, Asbury. *The Great Diamond Hoax and Other Stirring Episodes in the Life of Asbury Harpending*. Edited by James H. Wilkins. James H. Barry, 1913.

Janin, Henry. *A Brief Statement of My Part in the Unfortunate Diamond Affair*. San Francisco, 1873.

King, Clarence. *Mountaineering in the Sierra Nevada*. University of Nebraska Press, 1970. Originally published in Boston, 1872.

King, Clarence. *Systematic Geology*. Vol. 1 of *Report of the Geological Exploration of the Fortieth Parallel*. Washington, D.C., 1878.

Wilson, Allen D. "The Great California Diamond Mines: A True Story." *Overland Monthly* 43, no. 4 (Apr. 1904): 291–96.

SECONDARY SOURCES: BOOKS AND ARTICLES

Bancroft, Hubert Howe. *History of California*. Vol. 6, *1848–1850*. San Francisco, 1888.

Bartlett, Richard A. *Great Surveys of the American West*. University of Oklahoma Press, 1980.

Billman, Jon. "Tiffany's? Hardly. We Pick Ours Up in Laramie." *Outside*, Oct. 1, 1998. outsideonline.com/outdoor-adventure/tiffanys-hardly-we-pick-ours-laramie/.

Blair, Gerry. "Diamonds of the Wyoming Outback." *Lapidary Journal* 34, no. 2 (May 1980): 496–98.

Blakemore, Erin. "What Was It Like to Ride the Transcontinental Railroad?" History, Oct. 16, 2020. history.com/articles/transcontinental-railroad-experience.

Blust, Dick, Jr. "The Diamond Hoax: A Bonanza That Never Was." Wyoming History, Mar. 9, 2020. wyohistory.org/encyclopedia/diamond-hoax-bonanza-never-was.

Bowles, Samuel. *Our New West: Records of Travel*. Hartford, CT, 1869.

Bowles, Samuel. *The Pacific Railroad—Open: How to Go, What to See.* Boston, 1869.

Brands, H. W. *The Age of Gold: The California Gold Rush and the New American Dream.* Anchor Books, 2003.

Breihan, Carl W. *The Complete and Authentic Life of Jesse James.* Frederick Fell, 1953.

Cachinero, Eric. "Highwaymen: Nevada Outlaws Conducted the First Train Robbery in the West." *Nevada Magazine*, Mar.–Apr. 2018, 72–78.

Chernow, Ron. *Grant.* Penguin Books, 2017.

Considine, John L. "The Great Diamond Swindle." *Sunset*, Feb. 1924, 49–58.

Coolidge, Susan. "A Few Hints on the California Journey." *Scribner's Monthly*, May 1873, 25–31.

Crosby, Harry H. "The Great Dimond Fraud." *American Heritage*, Feb. 1956, 58–63, 100.

Cunningham, R. K. "200 Years of Illinois: Home of the Keeley Cure." University of Illinois Press online article, June 10, 2016. press.uillinois .edu/wordpress/200-years-of-illinois-home-of-the-keeley-cure/.

Daugherty, Greg. "This Defeated Presidential Candidate, Once the 'Best-Known Man in America,' Died in a Sanatorium Less Than a Month After Losing the Election." *Smithsonian*, Sept. 19, 2024. smithsonianmag .com/history/this-defeated-180985083/.

DeFord, Miriam Allen. *They Were San Franciscans.* Caxton Printers, 1947.

Dickson, Samuel. *Tales of San Francisco: Comprising "San Francisco Is Your Home," "San Francisco Kaleidoscope," and "The Streets of San Francisco."* Stanford University Press, 1957.

Emanuel, Harry. *Diamonds and Precious Stones: Their History, Value, and Distinguishing Characteristics*. London, 1865.

Evans, Albert S. *À la California: Sketches of Life in the Golden State*. San Francisco, 1873.

Farquhar, Peter. "Site of the Diamond Swindle of 1872." *Pacific Historical Society Quarterly* 42, no. 1 (Mar. 1963): 49–53.

Ferguson, H. N. "The Great Diamond Hoax of 1872 . . ." *Desert Magazine*, Feb. 1957, 4–7.

Fisher, Vardis, and Opal Laurel Holmes. *Gold Rushes and Mining Camps of the Early American West*. Caxton Printers, 1968.

Gilbert, Benjamin Franklin. "Kentucky Privateers in California." *Register of Kentucky State Historical Society* 38, no. 124 (July 1940): 256–66.

Gleason, Margaret. "Peshtigo Fire." Wisconsin Historical Society. wisconsinhistory.org/Records/Article/CS1750.

Hart, Matthew. *Diamond: The History of a Cold-Blooded Love Affair*. Plume, 2002.

Hilpert, Lowell S. "A Field Investigation of the Great Diamond Swindle." Unpublished paper, 1969–1972. Hilpert Papers.

Hilpert, Lowell S. "The Great Diamond Swindle: An American Classic." Unpublished manuscript, undated. Hilpert Papers.

Hittell, John S. *A History of the City of San Francisco and Incidentally of the State of California*. San Francisco, 1878.

Jackson, Helen Hunt. *Bits of Travel at Home*. Boston, 1878.

Kemp, Ben. "The Thin Blue Line." *Stories from Mt. McGregor* (blog). Grant Cottage, May 18, 2018. grantcottage.org/blog/2018/5/18/the-thin-blue-line.

Lavender, David. "How to Salt a Gold Mine." *American Heritage*, Apr. 1968, 65–71.

Lavender, David. *Nothing Seemed Impossible: William C. Ralston and Early San Francisco*. American West, 1975.

Lescohier, Roger. *Gold Giants of Grass Valley: History of the Empire and North Star Mines, 1850–1956*. Empire Mine Park Association, 1995.

Lewis, Oscar. *This Was San Francisco: Being First-Hand Accounts of the Evolution of One of America's Favorite Cities*. David McKay, 1962.

Liebling, A. J. "The American Golconda." Annals of Crime. *New Yorker*, Nov. 16, 1940, 49–62.

Linder, Douglas O. "Susan Anthony Trial (1873)." Famous Trials. UMKC School of Law. famous-trials.com/anthony.

Lineberry, Cate. "Diamonds Unearthed." *Smithsonian*, Dec. 2006. smithsonianmag.com/science-nature/diamonds-unearthed-141629226/.

Lyon, Fern. "The Reluctant Diamond Swindler." *New Mexico Magazine*, Oct. 1975, 12–13.

McGreevy, Nora. "In 1872, Susan B. Anthony Was Arrested for Voting 'Unlawfully.'" *Smithsonian*, Aug. 18, 2020. smithsonianmag.com/smart-news/why-susan-b-180975587/.

Moore, James Gregory. *King of the 40th Parallel: Discovery in the American West*. Stanford General Books, 2006.

Neville, Amelia Ransome. *The Fantastic City: Memoirs of the Social and Romantic Life of Old San Francisco*. Houghton Mifflin, 1932.

Plazak, Dan. *A Hole in the Ground with a Liar at the Top: Fraud and Deceit in the Golden Age of American Mining*. University of Utah Press, 2006.

Rae, W. F. *Westward by Rail: The New Route to the East*. New York, 1871.

Renda, Matthew. "Verdi's Historic Train Heist." *Tahoe Quarterly*, Summer 2018. tahoequarterly.com/looking-back/verdis-historic-train-heist.

Rosen, Fred. *Gold! The Story of the 1848 Gold Rush and How It Shaped a Nation.* Thunder's Mouth Press, 2005.

Rossi, Miriam. "How Can Graphite and Diamond Be So Different If They Are Both Composed of Pure Carbon?" *Scientific American*, Oct. 9, 2007. scientificamerican.com/article/how-can-graphite-and-diam/.

Sandweiss, Martha A. *Passing Strange: A Gilded Age Tale of Love and Deception Across the Color Line*. Penguin, 2009.

Smit, Karen V., and Steven B. Shirey. "Kimberlites: Earth's Diamond Delivery System." Diamonds from the Deep. *Gems & Gemology* 55, no. 2 (Summer 2019): 270–76.

Smith, Tom, III. "Jesse James in Iowa." *Annals of Iowa* 40, no. 5 (Summer 1970): 377–80.

Solly, Meilan. "When President Ulysses S. Grant Was Arrested for Speeding in a Horse-Drawn Carriage." *Smithsonian*, Mar. 31, 2023. smithsonianmag.com/smart-news/when-president-ulysses-s-grant-180981916/.

Trimble, Marshall. "Salting a Gold Mine." *True West Blog*, Jan. 10, 2017. truewestmagazine.com/article/salting-a-gold-mine/.

Wallentine, Anne. "There's a Better Way to Teach the California Gold Rush." *Smithsonian*, June 17, 2024. smithsonianmag.com/smithsonian-institution/theres-a-better-way-180984544/.

Wild, Peter. *Clarence King*. Boise State University, 1981.

Wilkins, Thurman. *Clarence King: A Biography*. Macmillan, 1958.

Wilson, Robert. *The Explorer King: Adventure, Science, and the Great Diamond Hoax—Clarence King in the Old West*. Shoemaker & Hoard, 2007.

Wilson, Robert. "The Great Diamond Hoax of 1872." *Smithsonian*, June 2004. smithsonianmag.com/history/the-great-diamond-hoax-2630188/.

Witt, Kathy. "A Colossal Con in Hardin Co." *Kentucky Living*, Mar. 28, 2017. kentuckyliving.com/archives/colossal-con-hardin-co.

Woodard, Bruce A. *Diamonds in the Salt*. Pruett, 1967.

Young, John P. *San Francisco: A History of the Pacific Coast Metropolis*. Vol. 1. S. J. Clarke, 1912.

NEWSPAPERS CONSULTED

Arizona Citizen (Tucson)

Courier-Journal (Louisville, Kentucky)

Daily Alta California (San Francisco)

Daily Bee (Sacramento, California)

Daily Denver Times

Daily Examiner (San Francisco)

Daily Independent (Laramie, Wyoming)

Daily Louisville Commercial (Kentucky)

Daily Rocky Mountain News (Denver)

Denver Post

Denver Tribune

Elizabethtown News (Kentucky)

Evening Bulletin (San Francisco)

Evening Star (Washington, D.C.)

Evening Telegraph (Philadelphia)

Gold Hill Daily News (Nevada)

Laramie Daily Sentinel (Wyoming)

Larue County Herald (Kentucky)

Mining and Scientific Press (San Francisco)

Mining Journal (London)

New Mexican (Santa Fe)

New York Times

New-York Tribune

Omaha Daily Bee (Nebraska)

Rochester Democrat and Chronicle (New York)

Sacramento Daily Union (California)

San Francisco Call

San Francisco Chronicle

St. Louis Globe-Democrat

Evening Mail (Stockton, California)

The Sun (New York)

The Times (London)

Weekly Arizonan (Tucson)

Weekly Miner (Prescott, Arizona)

Weekly New Mexican (Santa Fe)

White Oaks Eagle (New Mexico)

The World (New York)

ARCHIVAL SOURCES

Emmons, Samuel Franklin. Papers, 1725–1914. Library of Congress, Washington, D.C.

Geological Exploration of the Fortieth Parallel. Records. Copies of Letters and Reports Sent to the Chief of Engineers, Mar. 28, 1867–Jan. 18, 1879. National Archives and Records Administration, College Park, Maryland.

Harpending, Asbury. Papers, ca. 1862–1919. California Historical Society, San Francisco.

Hilpert, Lowell S. Papers, 1854–1992. American Heritage Center, University of Wyoming, Laramie.

King, Clarence. Papers, 1859–1902. Huntington Library, San Marino, California.

Lent v. P. Arnold, M. Arnold, J. Slack, et al. Hardin County Circuit Court records, Kentucky Archives Center.

United States v. Susan B. Anthony. Criminal Case Files, 1879–1910. Records of the District Courts of the United States, 1685–2009. National Archives. catalog.archives.gov/id/278294.

INDEX

AI scams, 199
Alcatraz Island, 29–30
American West. *See also specific states*
  California Gold Rush and, 14–16, 27–28
  Corydon, Iowa, bank robbery, 38–39
  diamonds in, 12, 44, 117
  Fortieth Parallel Survey in, 103–107, 110–112, 135, 142–144
  Lincoln's opposition to slavery in, 26
  Mexican-American War and, 19–20
  transcontinental railroad and, 33, 54–55, 88, 144, 199
  Verdi, Nevada, train robbery, 1–3
Anthony, Susan B., 56, 169–170
Arizona, diamond prospectors in, 117, 121, 139, 153, 173–174
Arkansas, Crater of Diamonds State Park in, 200
Arnold, Mary
  death of, 194
  diamond hoax and, 87–88
  leaving San Francisco, 36
  legal power over family finances, 35–36, 87, 189
  Lent's lawsuit against, 189–191
  marriage to Philip, 19
  returning to San Francisco, 64
  Roberts, payment from, 36, 87
  role in diamond hoax, 87–88
Arnold, Philip
  burying diamonds in basement of home, 195
  death of, 193–194
  dispute and shootout with Holdsworth, 193–194
  early life of, 19, 45–47
  impersonators of, 133
  investors' trip to diamond mine with, 66–67, 69–73, 75–78
  Lent's lawsuit against, 189–191
  marriage to Mary, 19
  newspapers interviewing, 119–121
  New York City trip with investors, 54–55, 58–60

Arnold, Philip (*continued*)
payment to Harpending, 174–176
proceeds from diamond hoax, 62, 83–84, 91, 191
refusal to sell diamond mine, 34–35, 53
return to diamond mine to retrieve diamonds, 200
salting accusations against, 186–188
salting diamond mine, 87–91
secrecy of diamond mine location, 12, 20–21, 35
selling diamond mine, 62, 83–84
silver mine, claims of finding, 191–192
storing diamonds in Robert's safe, 7–13
survey of diamond mine and, 100–101, 113–114, 133
suspected of mine salting, 136–137, 182–185

Bank of California, 34
bank robberies, 38–39
Barlow, Samuel, 59–60, 64
barometers, 105
"Ben Butler" (sea lion), 33
Berry, J. F., 162–165, 172–173
Black Americans
Black police officer ticketing Grant, 92–94
civil rights and, 56, 60–61
hired for survey of diamond mine, 113–114
interracial marriage and, 197–198
Reconstruction and, 55–56
slavery and, 26
voting rights under Fifteenth Amendment, 56
Blust, Dick, Jr., 206–207
Brewer, William, 106
bribes, 60–61
A Brief Statement of My Part in the Unfortunate Diamond Affair (Janin), 181–182
Butler, Benjamin, 33, 60–61, 66, 188

California. *See also* San Francisco
Bank of California, 34
California Gold Rush, 14–16, 27–28
Harpending and Rubery's piracy off coast of, 27–31
carats, 163
Chicago Great Fire (1871), 56
Chinese immigrants, 33
Civil War, 26–27, 30–31
Cleveland, Charles, 127–128, 130–131, 178
Colorado
diamond companies in, 122
diamond mine in. *See* Great Diamond Hoax
Diamond Peak in, 76, 201, 205–207, *206–207*
diamond prospectors in, 117, 128
Congress
Fortieth Parallel Survey, financing for, 110
mining laws and, 60–61, 66
on sovereignty of Indian tribes, 55
Cooper, J. B., 45, 184
Copeland, Ada, 197–198

Corydon, Iowa bank robbery (1871), 38–39
Crater of Diamonds State Park, Arkansas, 200

Davis, A. J., 1–3
diamond experts, 18, 59–60, 89, 136–137, 199
diamond fever, 83, 122–123, 157
diamond mine. *See* Great Diamond Hoax
Diamond Peak, Colorado, 76, 201, 205–207, *206–207*
diamonds. *See also* Great Diamond Hoax
  in American West, 12, 44, 117
  carats and, 163
  Crater of Diamonds State Park, Arkansas, 200
  digital records of origins, 199–200
  discoveries around the world, 43
  formation of, 41–42
  Mohs scale and, 41, 45–46
  quartz mistaken for, 17, 44, 139–140, 210, *210*
  rough diamonds, 11, 18, 46–47, 199
  testing, 46, 139–140
Diamonds and Precious Stones: Their History, Value, and Distinguishing Characteristics, 46–47
Diamonds in the Salt (Woodard), 208
Dodge, George S., 52, 54–55, 66–67, 69–73, 75–78

Elizabethtown, Kentucky
  Arnold hiring mining crew from, 113–114, 123
  Arnold's place of birth, 19
  Arnolds' return to, 91, 100
  Gilded Age office building in, 192
Emmons, Samuel
  discovery of diamond hoax, 159–165
  search for diamond mine, 135, 142–146, 150–157
  survey of American West, 106, 111
  warning others of diamond hoax, 172

Fifteenth Amendment, 56
Fortieth Parallel Survey, 110–112
  conditions endured by King and crew, 106, 111
  King as Geologist in Charge, 103–107, 110
  learning news of diamond mine inspected by Janin, 111, 135, 142–144
  team's scientific investigation of mine location, 159–165
  team's search for diamond mine, 149–157
Fourteenth Amendment, 56
Fox, George W., 117, 121

Gardner, James, 135, 142–146
geology. *See* surveying land
Gilded Age, 58–59
Gillette, Martin F., 127, 142
gold
  California Gold Rush, 14–16, 27–28
  Harpending and Rubery's plan to steal, 27–31

gold (*continued*)
  in medicines, 86
  salting of mines, 85–86
  Sutter's discovery as start of Gold Rush, 14–15
  Verdi train robbery and theft of, 1–3
Gold Cure (fake medicine), 86
Grant, Ulysses S., 55–56, 66, 92–94, 170
Gray, Mike
  expedition saved from starvation, 173–174
  leading decoy expedition, 125–129
  lost on purpose, 134
Great Chicago Fire (1871), 56
Great Diamond Hoax
  Arnold and Slack's proceeds from, 35, 62, 81, 83–84, 91, 191
  Arnold's defense against mine "salting" accusations, 186–188
  Arnold's payment to Harpending and, 174–176
  author's visit to diamond mine, 205–210, *206–207*, *209–210*
  criminal investigation of, 184
  decoy survey expedition and, 123–129, 134, 173–174
  diamond authentication by jewelers, 17–18, 54, 59–60, 89
  diamond hoax, discovery of, 159–168
  diamond hunters searching for mine, 99, 116–123, 149, 200–201
  discovery of diamond mine, 7–13, 16–17
  expected profits from, 115–116
  Fortieth Parallel team's scientific investigation of mine location, 159–165
  Fortieth Parallel team's search for diamond mine, 135, 142–146, 149–157
  investors' interest in diamond mine, 52–55, 58–60
  investors' trip to diamond mine, 66–67, 69–73, 75–78, 81
  Janin confirming diamond hoax, 171–172
  Janin's official geologist report on, 82–83
  legal claim to land and, 35, 54, 60, 77–78, 98, 124, 138, 148
  Lent's lawsuit against Arnold for, 189–191
  money lost in, 180–181
  newspapers reporting on, 96–97, 177–180
  public interest in diamond mine, 95–97
  sale of shares in diamond mine, 34–35, 62, 83–84
  salting the mine, 85–91, 136–137, 178, 182–185
  secrecy of mine location, 12, 20–21, 35, 96, 98–99, 116–118, 121, 145–148
  survey of diamond mine and, 100–101, 113–116, 127–131, 138, 141–148
  suspicions of diamond hoax, 136–137, 140–141, 182–185

The Great Diamond Hoax and Other Stirring Incidents in the Life of Asbury Harpending (Harpending), 201–202
Greeley, Horace, 59, 94, 170

Harpending, Asbury
- Arnold's payment to, 174–176
- arrest of, 29–31
- attempt to buy diamond mine, 34–35
- Civil War and, 26–27
- coded messages of, 79–81
- death of, 203
- decoy survey expedition and, 123–127
- diamond hoax, confirming, 171–172
- diamond hoax, learning of, 166–168
- diamond mine, purchasing, 53, 83–84
- early life of, 25–31
- leaving San Francisco after diamond hoax, 202–203
- memoir by, 201–202
- mining company ownership of, 95–98
- money lost in diamond hoax, 180–181
- New York City trip with investors, 54–55, 57–60
- piracy off coast of California and, 27–31
- receiving rough diamonds from Arnold and Slack, 47–53
- return to California, 23–24, 32–34
- on richness of diamond field, 83
- Roberts's telegrams on diamond mine to, 21–23, 65
- role in diamond hoax, 81, 175, 185, 189–190, 201–202
- survey of diamond mine and, 115, 128
- suspicions of diamond hoax, 136–137, 140–141
- trip to diamond mine, 66–67, 69–73, 75–78

Hartley, Don, 205–207
Hilpert, Lowell S., 201
Holdsworth, Harry, 193–194

Indian Appropriations Act (1871), 55
internet scams, 198–199

James, Jesse, 38–39
Janin, Henry
- defense after diamond hoax, 181–183, 187
- diamond hoax, learning of, 166–168
- hired as mining engineer for diamond investors, 61–62
- mining company ownership of, 97
- official report on diamond mine, 82
- reputation of, 61, 82, 111, 135, 143
- return to diamond mine with King, 171–172, 176
- rumored murder of, 123
- sale of diamond company stock, 123–124
- survey of diamond mine and, 114–116, 143–144
- trip to diamond mine, 66–67, 69–73, 75–78

jewelers
- diamond authentication by Harpending with Tiffany, 54, 59–60
- diamond authentication by Roberts with, 17–18
- diamond hoaxes uncovered by, 139–140
- in Europe, Arnold and Slack purchasing diamonds from, 88, 89, 136–137, 140–141
- modern diamond authentication by, 199–200

Jones as Gray's assistant, 127–128, 173–174

Kentucky. *See also* Elizabethtown
- Harpending's place of birth, 25
- Harpending returning to, 202–203

King, Clarence
- career following diamond hoax, 197–198
- diamond hoax, discovery of, 159–165
- diamond hoax, sharing news of, 165–168
- diamond mine and, 135
- early life of, 109–110
- as hero, 179
- lightning strike on, 106
- return to diamond mine with Janin, 171–172, 176
- search for diamond mine, 149–152, 154–157
- survey of American West, 103–107, 110–112. *See also* Fortieth Parallel Survey

land surveys. *See* surveying land

Law, William, 29–30

Lent, William
- on diamond hoax, 140–141
- investing in diamond mine, 52
- lawsuit against Arnold, 189–191
- mining company ownership of, 95–96
- New York City trip with investors, 54–55
- survey of diamond mine and, 146–147

Lincoln, Abraham, 26, 30–31

MacIntyre, Lloyd, 113

Madoff, Bernie, 198

Marryatt, James, 104

Marshall, James, 14–15

May, Mary. *See* Arnold, Mary

McCague, William, 192

McClellan, George, 59, 96

Mexican–American War, 19–20

Miner, Tom, 117–118, 121–122, 153

mineral hardness scale, 41, 45–46

mining
- California Gold Rush and, 14–16, 27–28
- for diamonds. *See* Great Diamond Hoax
- laws on, 60–61, 66
- salting of gold mines, 85–86

Mining and Scientific Press, 46

Mining Law (1872), 66

Mohs, Friedrich, 45–46

Mohs scale, 41, 45–46

Morse code, 79

Native Americans
  Gold Rush and, 15
  Gray's decoy expedition and, 173
  land taken from, 55
  Mexican–American War and territory of, 20
  Utes in Wyoming, 66
Nevada, Verdi train heist in (1870), 1–3
New Mexico
  diamond prospectors in, 121–122, 128–129
  silver mine in, 19
newspapers reporting on Great Diamond Hoax, 96–97, 177–180
New York City, diamond mine investors' trip to, 54–55, 57–60

Original Diamond Discovery and Mining Company, 122, 153

Pavellas, Ron, 203–204
Peshtigo fire (1871), 56–57
piracy, 27–31

quartz, 17, 44, 139–140, 210, *210*

racism, 56. *See also* Black Americans
railroads
  train robberies, 1–3
  transcontinental, 33, 54–55, 88, 144, 199
Ralston, William
  attempt to buy diamond mine, 34–35
  diamond hoax, learning of, 166–167
  Harpending's coded message to, 79
  mining company ownership of, 95–96
  money lost in diamond hoax, 181
  search for Arnold and Slack, 185
Reconstruction period, 55–56
Roberts, George
  attempt to buy diamond mine, 34–35
  career following diamond hoax, 196
  decoy survey expedition and, 123–124
  desire for location of diamond mine, 20–21
  diamond authentication and, 17–18
  diamond discovery and, 7–13, 16–17, 87
  diamond hoax, learning of, 166–168
  early life of, 15–16
  financial troubles of, 16, 63–64
  Gold Rush and, 15–16
  on location of diamond mine, 121–122
  as mark for diamond hoax, 87, 184
  mining company ownership of, 95–98
  money lost in diamond hoax, 180–181
  payment to Mary Arnold, 36, 87
  survey of diamond mine and, 114–116, 127–130, 138, 141–142, 147–148
  telegrams to Harpending on diamond mine, 21–23, 65
Rothschild, Lionel de, 83

Rothschild family, 96
rough diamonds, 11, 18, 46–47, 88–89, 199
Rubery, Alfred
  accepting Harpending's money from Arnold, 174–176
  arrest of, 29–31
  Civil War and, 26–27
  early life of, 26–31
  interest in diamond find, 23–24
  New York City trip with investors, 54–55
  piracy off coast of California and, 27–31
  survey expedition lead by, 127, 129–131, 138, 141–142
  trip to diamond mine, 66–67, 69–73, 75–78, 81
rubies
  found at diamond mine, 51, 75–76, 141, 157
  garnets mistaken for, 44
  Mohs scale and, 46

salting of mines
  Arnold accused of, 186–188
  Arnold and Slack suspected of, 136–137, 182–185
  fake gold mines and, 85–86
  Great Diamond Hoax and, 87–91, 136–137, 178, 182–185
San Francisco, California
  Chinatown in, 33
  Gold Rush and, 15
  Harpending and Rubery's plan to steal gold from, 27–31
  history of, 5–6, 32–33
San Francisco and New York Mining and Commercial Company, 95–98, 124, 140–141. *See also* Great Diamond Hoax
scams
  Arnold and Slack's plan, 87–91. *See also* Great Diamond Hoax
  internet, 198–199
  Madoff, 198
  salting to create fake gold mines, 85–86
Slack, John
  career following diamond hoax, 195–196
  early life of, 19–20
  investors' trip to diamond mine with, 66–67, 69–73, 75–78, 81
  keeping diamond mine a secret, 12, 20–21
  proceeds from diamond mine sale, 35, 53, 81
  salting diamond mine, 87–91
  selling share of diamond mine, 34–35, 53
  storing diamonds in Robert's safe, 7–13
  suspected of mine salting, 136–137, 184–185
slavery, 26
Stanton, Elizabeth Cady, 56
surveying
  diamond mine and, 100–101, 114–116, 127–131, 138, 141–148
  Fortieth Parallel Survey of American West, 103–107, 110–112, 142
Sutter, John, 14–15

Sweetwater County Historical
Museum, Wyoming, 206–207

telegrams, 21–22, 79–80, 165–166
Thompson, Ira Anna, 31
Tiffany, Charles Lewis, 54, 59–60, 89
train robberies, 1–3
transcontinental railroad, 33, 54–55,
88, 144, 199

Ute Indians, 66

Verdi train heist, Nevada (1870), 1–3
volcanic eruptions, 42
voting rights, 56, 169–170

West, William, 92–94
Western United States. *See* American
West
Wilson, A. D., 111, 150, 154–157,
159–165
women's suffrage movement and right
to vote, 56, 169–170
Wood, W. D., 189–191
Woodard, Bruce A., 195,
208
Wyoming Territory
diamond mine in. *See* Great
Diamond Hoax
Native Americans in, 66
women's right to vote in, 56